BE AGILE

A simple, proven blueprint
for mastering agile

BY TERRY HAAYEMA

BE Agile
Copyright © 2022 By Terry Haayema
First published in 2022

Print: 978-1-922456-95-3
E-book: 978-1-922456-96-0
Hardback: 978-1-922456-94-6

All rights reserved. No part of this book may be reproduced, stored in a retrieval system, or transmitted by any means (electronic, mechanical, photocopying, recording, or otherwise) without written permission from the author.

Because of the dynamic nature of the Internet, any web addresses or links contained in this book may have changed since publication and may no longer be valid. The information in this book is based on the author's experiences and opinions. The views expressed in this book are solely those of the author and do not necessarily reflect the views of the publisher; the publisher hereby disclaims any responsibility for them.

The author of this book does not dispense any form of medical, legal, financial, or technical advice either directly or indirectly. The intent of the author is solely to provide information of a general nature to help you in your quest for personal development and growth. In the event you use any of the information in this book, the author and the publisher assume no responsibility for your actions. If any form of expert assistance is required, the services of a competent professional should be sought.

Publishing information
Publishing, design, and production facilitated by Passionpreneur Publishing, A division of Passionpreneur Organization Pty Ltd, ABN: 48640637529

www.PassionpreneurPublishing.com
Melbourne, VIC | Australia

Contents

Acknowledgements		vii
Introduction		ix
Pushing Rocks Uphill		xi
Rolling Snowballs Downhill		xix
Section 1	**Being Agile**	1
Chapter 1	What is Agile?	7
Chapter 2	A Venn Diagram of Agility	17
Chapter 3	Purpose	29
Chapter 4	Flow	35
Chapter 5	Change	45
Chapter 6	Learning or Winning	59
Chapter 7	Growth is Not Comfortable	65
Chapter 8	Making Sense	73
Chapter 9	Cognitive Biases	81
Chapter 10	Feedback	115

Chapter 11:	You Can't See the Label From Inside the Jar	125
Summary – Being Agile		135

Section 2	**Doing Agile**	141
Chapter 1	Setting Goals	145
Chapter 2	Backlogs	169
Chapter 3	Estimation	179
Chapter 4	Prioritisation	197
Chapter 5	Experimentation	213
Chapter 6	Make Work Visible	231
Chapter 7	Incremental and Iterative	239
Chapter 8	Outcome Over Output	245
Chapter 9	Timeboxing	251
Chapter 10	Stop Starting and Start Finishing	257
Chapter 11	Meaningful Metrics and How to Use Them	263
Chapter 12	Fail Fast	269
Chapter 13	Continuous Improvement & Compounding Interest	279
Chapter 14	Deliberate Practice	297
Summary – Doing Agile		301
How agile am I? Worksheet		307

Conclusion	311
Still want more?	315
About the author	319

I dedicate this book to my wonderful family, my gorgeous wife Mary, and my sons Elden and Callum. You have provided unconditional support as I went through this writing journey, creating a space that allowed me to focus and be creative.

You are my wellspring of joy and my happy place, I love you!

Acknowledgements

I'd like to acknowledge all the people who have helped me to learn and to grow in my understanding of agility to the point where I was able to author this book.

Many of the masters in the agile arena, freely offer their tools and techniques for everyone to learn and enjoy for free, most of the tools, models, techniques and approaches in this book were developed by incredible people who have all contributed to the immense body of knowledge that makes up agility today. To all the agile masters in the world, I thank you.

The agile community is large, vibrant and diverse with a deep desire to learn, share and grow together. To the many people in that community that I have shared a learning space with, I thank you.

To my beautiful wife Mary, whose unflinching support throughout this entire writing experience kept me going through the difficulties and to my sons Elden and Callum who provided motivation and a sounding board, I thank you.

To you my readers who will take the ideas presented in this book, use them to make your work and your lives better and share them with others, evolving them further to suit your own context, I thank you.

Introduction

Congratulations on picking up this book. No matter where you are in your knowledge of "agile" this book is for you.

If you're new to agile, you will love this book. You'll learn what agile is and ways you can apply it to how you think and how you work. You'll find this book crammed full of new approaches to dealing with complex situations that will bring joy to your life.

Being new to agile many of the concepts and models presented here will be new to you and may sound a little strange, some of them can be counter intuitive. If you feel a gut-level response that a concept is simply wrong and could never work for you, then it might just be the concept you need the most. That said, my suggestion would be to start with the concepts that feel the most valuable and easily adopted, they will get you started and help you to build confidence in your ability to adopt agility.

If you've heard about agile but are unsure what it means to you, you will love this book. You'll find new levels of understanding for all the tools and techniques you're already familiar with and hopefully a few new ones as well that will add new strings to your bow. I hope reading this book brings joy to your life.

Maybe you're a people leader or a project manager and you're hearing that there are no managers and no projects in agile. You might be concerned about your future and worried that your role will no longer exist when your company adopts agile. Rest assured, leadership is still required, and project management skills are still valuable in agile organisations, you just apply them differently. The best thing you can do is to learn as much as you an about agile approaches, tools and techniques.

If you're experienced with agile you will love this book. You'll find that the experiences shared and the ways the tools and techniques are explained brings new levels of nuance that you can use to uplift your agile practice, so it brings even more joy to your life.

As an experienced agile practitioner, most of the concepts and models will be familiar, I hope I am able to expose a new dimension for at least some of them that helps you to enhance your practice by seeing them differently through another view of their underlying intent.

Pushing Rocks Uphill

How I fought the system and lost

Have you ever felt that the system was against you? That you were struggling against the system in a battle of wits that was impossible to win? I did, and I have the scars to prove it.

Back in the 1990s, I was managing the delivery of technology projects for large organisations, juggling impossible timelines in an environment where the cost of the project was more important than the people doing the work. I felt there had to be a better way, but I had no idea what it could be.

I remember the day I first encountered agile as if it was yesterday. I didn't know at the time, but it was going to have an enormous impact on me.

> IF SOMEONE OFFERS YOU AN AMAZING OPPORTUNITY AND YOU'RE NOT SURE YOU CAN DO IT, SAY YES – THEN LEARN HOW TO DO IT LATER.
> *Sir Richard Branson*

BE AGILE

My manager told me we were 'going agile' and gave me a book to read.

The book was "Agile Software Development with Scrum" by Ken Schwaber and Mike Beedle. It's a terrific book and I devoured it in a weekend.

Suddenly, I was a Scrum Master, even though I received no training and had no idea what that meant.

> THE SCRUM MASTER IS ACCOUNTABLE FOR THE SCRUM TEAM'S EFFECTIVENESS. THEY DO THIS BY ENABLING THE SCRUM TEAM TO IMPROVE ITS PRACTICES, WITHIN THE SCRUM FRAMEWORK.
> *The Scrum Guide*

I remember feeling like I'd been set adrift: I'd been delivering software for a long time and was confident in my abilities, but this new Scrum Master role was entirely unknown. Sure, I'd read the book and knew the basic mechanics of the framework, but most of it was completely unfamiliar, counter-intuitive and felt like voodoo.

At the time, I thought I was doing a decent job. I did all the activities and ticked all the boxes, but as I look back now – and with the benefit of hindsight – I know I was rubbish at it.

After many months of struggling to come to terms with my new situation, I started to understand some of the intent behind the practices and developed some small level of confidence. Solving people problems is certainly more complex and more difficult than solving technical problems, but it was also much more rewarding, and I came to enjoy the Scrum Master aspect of my work more than the software development part.

As my grasp of agile practices and ability to operate with agility grew, I came to love the fact that it refocused on the people and the outcomes – instead of the cost and the output.

Through my work as a Scrum Master, I learned about the practices in agile methodologies and became proficient in teaching and training teams how to adopt those practices. I became confident in adapting the practices to suit individual circumstances without breaking the underlying intent.

Enjoying the role and starting to understand how much I didn't know, I developed a hunger for learning and a passion for helping those in my team to learn. I set about reading everything I could get my hands on and doing every course I could enrol in.

With my budding understanding of agile practices, I became a Product Owner at a major beverages company. I thought I knew enough about agile and understood the role well enough, but once again, I was out of my depth and barely able to stay afloat.

> THE PRODUCT OWNER IS ACCOUNTABLE FOR MAXIMIZING THE VALUE OF THE PRODUCT RESULTING FROM THE WORK OF THE SCRUM TEAM.
>
> The Scrum Guide

About a year into the role, I could start to show real improvement in the team's ability to deliver customer and business value, and I had a fair enough grasp on the activities and functions of the role, even though I was still operating like a Project Manager. I'd like to think I was fairly good at it, but I certainly wasn't great.

That was when I discovered the wonderful community that was building up around agile and I started to engage in different groups and meetups, attending presentations and participating in workshops.

My previous passion for learning became turbo-charged. Here was a community of like-minded people who were happy to give of their time and themselves to share their learning and experience with others for the sheer joy of helping others.

I learned about agile planning techniques and ways to map out a feature or requirement so that it is easier to break it down to small pieces and techniques to assess priorities, so that we were always working on the most valuable things.

Over the next couple of years, I had many lightbulb moments that each blew my mind in ways I could not have previously imagined.

One of those lightbulb moments came when a team member asked why we were working on a particular feature. I couldn't answer beyond the fact that management had requested it. I reflected afterwards and realised that I had not been operating as a Product Owner with real ownership and accountability for decisions about value, but simply taking orders from management and passing them on to the team. I learned the importance of saying no as a Product Owner.

It would take a few more years before I mastered the art of saying no, but it had an immediate uplift in how I was perceived by leaders because it demonstrated to them that I was taking ownership and accountability. Leaders stopped telling us what to do and started listening to what we thought.

Another 'aha' moment came when I found a way to report on the real value delivered by the team. They had been struggling under stifling micromanagement in a culture of command and control with all their decisions being made by their managers. Focus had always been on cost; delivering on time and within budget seemed like the only important things. When I was able to attach an actual dollar value to what the team delivered, the thumbscrews came off. Everything swiftly changed and the team became empowered to make some of their own decisions and were finally allowed to take some level of control over their own destiny. The additional autonomy motivated the team even more and their performance improved dramatically in a very short period of time, simply through being able to prove how valuable they were.

Through a series of workshops and learning events, I found myself connecting with elements of agile that were new to me because I had been doing agile in a way that focused on the activities and functions of the work, not the intent or the mindset behind it.

I had been doing the job exactly as it was described – but I was missing the point entirely. After this, agility opened up before me: it was so much more than a set of practices or any specific activities – it was a way of being and

> AGILE IS AN ATTITUDE, NOT A TECHNIQUE WITH BOUNDARIES. AN ATTITUDE HAS NO BOUNDARIES.
> Alistair Cockburn.

a mindset that resonated with me in a way that none of my previous work ever did.

A few years later, I took a job as an agile coach and my learning journey accelerated once again.

Once again, I was in a job I understood the function of, but had very little capability in the execution of it or understanding of what it really meant.

My experience with being a Scrum Master and a Product Owner allowed me to help people with the 'what' and the 'why' of their work as well as the 'how' of getting that work done efficiently, but was still more focused on doing agile practices rather than living an agile mindset (more on that later!).

Through my work as an agile coach, my understanding of the importance of culture in any group grew, and I slanted my learning towards understanding and influencing group dynamics within human systems.

A couple of years into the role, I stumbled across, "The Goal" by Eliyahu M. Goldratt. It was written in 1984 (before agile was even a thing), and brings together so many of the agile techniques I had been practicing in a way that allowed everything to click in my mind. Suddenly I understood a much bigger picture about one of the hidden objectives of being agile: to optimise the entire system for the effective delivery of valuable customer outcomes.

My eyes were opened in a new way. It wasn't about the practices or making teams go faster; it was about the big picture and how to make adjustments in a complex adaptive human system.

Agile isn't about individual practices, methodologies or frameworks. It is about how you put it all together. When you bring it all together, agile really is bigger than the sum of the parts.

When that combined with organisational culture, making the flow of value visible, agile planning and delivery techniques and the ability to make empirical decisions based on real metrics, I realised I had the makings of a new approach to applying agile ways of working that would help not just the people doing the work, but their customers and leaders as well.

After testing the approach with the teams I was working with, the results were staggering.

One team was working on a reporting feature that would normally have taken them 6 weeks. In applying agile approaches, they were able to see their overall system differently, which allowed them to deliver the entire solution in 3 hours!

Another team struggling with never-ending changes in requirements was able to apply some of the agile planning techniques and complete their first successful release in 2 years!

To get to this point in my career and learning journey, I've read literally hundreds and hundreds of the best books in the industry, attended and spoken at dozens of conferences all over the world, been a conference organiser, and been certified in just about everything agile you can imagine. I've boiled those down through hard-earned experience delivering difficult projects to bring you the simple, proven system you'll discover in the rest of this book.

My name is Terry Haayema, and my personal purpose is, "To help people see differently, so they find joy." That's why I've written this book.

If this book helps you to see something differently and it brings you happiness, then my purpose has been achieved.

Let's get started!

Rolling Snowballs Downhill

How small changes add up to big improvements

The meaning of agile will be revealed as we go through this journey together, but for now let's just say that agile is about effective ways of conceiving, planning, organising, and doing work. An agile mindset fosters learning, collaboration and approaching large complex outcomes as a series of small simple actions.

Are you doing agile without really understanding why?

Is your team complaining that there are too many meetings?

Do your requirements keep changing, even after they have been signed off?

Do your stakeholders complain that the team is slow and expensive?

Does everything feel like it's harder than it needs to be?

If you answered yes to any of the above questions, then you may be in a similar situation to where I was when I started my journey: you're pushing rocks uphill.

Read on! By the end of this chapter, I'll show you how you can eliminate those problems with a simple and proven technique that not only improves your performance, but also makes work more fun.

Agile is not a new way of working

When most people first come across agile, they might only consider it as a way of working to make teams go faster. Some organisations even describe their attempts at adopting agile as, "New Ways of Working" and you see all sorts of crazy acronyms like WoW, NWoW, or EWoW.

If you think of agile as a way of working, you're missing the point. And while you'll still get some benefit from adopting the practices, the real benefits of agility will be lost.

I've seen it happen so many times: the results of adopting an agile practice without an agile mindset. At some point there will be pressure or difficulty and the practice will be changed or abandoned. When an agile practice is changed without having the agile mindset or understanding the intent of the practice, it becomes broken and can end up being even worse than what was in place before agile came along.

Creating or adopting a new set of practices or being more prescriptive in 'Ways of Working' is not the solution you're searching for. Training teams in how to adopt agile practices will not create a culture of high performance. Writing a new set of 'Playbooks' will not overcome your struggles.

Agile makes problems visible

While 'doing agile' won't solve your problems, it does have the potential to make your problems visible, which can make it very uncomfortable for people adopting it as just a way to speed up teams.

The way to deal with it is to accept that agile is not a way of working, a new way of working, or an enterprise way of working. It is a way of *being*.

> IF YOUR ORGANISATION DOESN'T LIKE TRUTH AND HONESTY, IT PROBABLY WON'T LIKE AGILE.
> Henrik Kniberg.

Agile cannot be adopted as a set of practices, implemented as a bunch of extra meetings, or described in a set of 'Playbooks.' Agile is a mindset. Changing mindsets is not something you adopt through a change management exercise; it is planted as a seed of understanding with the emphasis on the *why* and then nurtured with small ongoing improvements.

Agility is something you evolve into, not something you adopt. It is nourished or starved through the culture of the team and those surrounding it.

This book won't suddenly transform you into an agile individual, but it will offer new ways of doing things, different approaches to dealing with problems and opportunities to learn and grow.

Even after reading this book and the many others published on the topic of agility, you will still have further to go on your journey of learning and understanding. You will only start to develop that deeper understanding when you put the ideas presented here and elsewhere into practice, and experience how they work and what it feels like.

After many years of delivering projects the hard way and having been through an apprenticeship of fire into the new world of agile "ways of working", I was disillusioned and unhappy. But I knew that there was a seed of something great at the core of agile that just needed to be nurtured to grow into something that could help people to see all this differently.

I had seen firsthand just how powerful agile could be in helping people find joy in their work and belonging to an awesome team. I had also seen how teams people enjoyed being on dramatically outperformed those that were just a group of people working on the same things.

I had also witnessed teams where pretty much the same practices were adopted, but the improvements were negligible. And so it became clear that it wasn't the practices themselves that were turning some teams into a formidable force for delivering customer value and leaving other teams feeling like they were stuck having too many meetings.

I needed to find the secret sauce that turbo-charged the high performing teams and create a way for all teams to apply it.

You can't adopt Agile, you evolve into it

I already knew that agile was a mindset and that the culture of the team and those supporting them was the determining factor in whether agile would take hold and flourish or wither and die.

I understood this 'on paper' but I came to deeply understand: mindset and culture are not just the most important aspects of agility, they are *the sum total of everything agile*.

All agile practices attempt to establish a deliberate set of behaviours that will eventually evolve the mindset and culture. But this can be thwarted when the mindset and culture within and around the team are centred on people doing what they're told or just doing their jobs. The team ends up following the practices because they were told to, so it becomes nothing more than a set of tasks. The pervasive external culture wins, and agile suffers.

Changing mindset and culture means evolving the mindset and culture of the individuals in the team and those surrounding them, including their leaders, stakeholders, and the teams they interact with.

When I think of mindset, I think of a set of mental patterns that have been built up over a person's entire life. A mindset cannot be upgraded for a better one in one go, the way a phone app can be upgraded. To influence a person's mindset, you need to create a new mental pattern and give that pattern time to strengthen while understanding that the old patterns are still there. It will take time before the new patterns get strong enough to influence how the person operates.

When I think of culture, I think of all our behaviours, our interactions and the idea of 'how we do things around here.' Like mindset, you can't adopt a new culture and replace an existing culture in one go. To evolve a culture, you need to create small positive habits that are repeated often enough to become part of our very being.

It starts with individuals

The traditional way to consider 'agile transformations' was to focus on the team. But teams, business units and entire organisations are made up of individuals. And my big realisation was that mindset and culture need changes in the individual if we want to transform teams and organisations.

We couldn't just focus solely on the team anymore, and this was the most important belief to change. Instead, we need to focus on the individual.

Teams are groups of individuals, so if we can help each of the team members to develop an agile mindset, then the agile practices will make more sense and it will be easier for them to deliver better quality faster and enjoy their work as they were going about it.

My approach shifted to supporting individual agility and helping one person at a time to develop a more agile mindset and culture, which evolved into helping people take an agile perspective into everything they do.

It has evolved over time through being tested with a wide variety of people and teams and has withstood many different situations and working environments.

I call it the snowball technique because just like a snowball, once you release it, snow accumulates as it rolls until it is powerful enough to smash through any obstacle in its path.

Throwing a single snowball down a mountain can start an avalanche.

Small improvements with a clear intent

Remember that you cannot fully understand agility by simply reading about it. Think of agility as being a little bit mysterious. Consider it to be like a dark art

> THE GREATEST DANGER IN TIMES OF TURBULENCE IS NOT THE TURBULENCE; IT IS TO ACT WITH YESTERDAY'S LOGIC.
> Peter Drucker

that you need to be initiated into. This will help you to maintain an observer's approach and learning mindset, developing a deeper understanding as you experience it directly.

Throughout it all, the underlying intention is to start small: embed each change with intent and an understanding of why you are doing it so that it can form a solid component of your way of working that supports the agile mindset and culture.

Just like we want a snowball to be small and firmly packed before we roll it down the hill, the subtle shifts in habits embedded with intention will establish behaviours. When the intention is supported by repeating those behaviours, they become beliefs. Beliefs underpin behaviours and repeated behaviours are the foundation of who we become.

As you progress, choose small improvements that eventually add up until your team becomes a well-oiled delivery machine, able to overcome any obstacle in their path.

Once your foundation is in place, the process becomes easy and natural and as your improvements accumulate, you will find that is has become part of your team's DNA and people will look forward to it.

The snowball technique is framework agnostic: no matter how you go about your work today. you will benefit from applying it. If your team or the teams you lead are practicing Scrum, Kanban, XP or even working in a traditional project flow, you can use this technique without adding any tasks, meetings, or activities to the team's workload.

While there is a lot of material in the chapters that follow about how to complete agile practices, the outcome of applying these practices with intention will allow you to BE Agile.

SECTION 1
BEING AGILE

BE AGILE

*To be uncertain is to be uncomfortable,
but to be certain is to be ridiculous.*

— Chinese Proverb

***

You improvise. You adapt. You overcome.

— Clint Eastwood as Sergeant Highway
in Heartbreak Ridge

***

*A good plan violently executed now
is better than a perfect plan executed next week.*

— General George S. Patton

***

*Opportunity is missed by most people because it is
dressed in overalls and looks like work.*

— Thomas Edison

An agile individual holds two core characteristics: they are clear about what agile means to them, while also understanding that no matter how well you think you know it there are deeper meanings to be discovered and an ever-increasing number of ways to apply it.

Even people who work in the field struggle with a concise definition of what agile is. Ask 10 Agile Coaches what agile is and you'll get 11 different responses.

Agile is both simple and complex.

The simplicity of agile comes from its beginnings in 2001 when 17 software professionals gathered at the Snowbird ski resort in the Wasatch mountains of Utah to discuss alternatives to the slow, painful, documentation-heavy, tightly-controlled and prone to failure processes that were popular at the time.

They created, 'The Agile Manifesto,' a simple declaration of 4 values and 12 principles that are presented in 2 very simple web pages.

https://agilemanifesto.org/

***

Manifesto for Agile Software Development

We are uncovering better ways of developing software by doing it and helping others do it. Through this work we have come to value:

Individuals and interactions over processes and tools
Working software over comprehensive documentation
Customer collaboration over contract negotiation
Responding to change over following a plan

That is, while there is value in the items on the right, we value the items on the left more.

***

The Agile Manifesto was born in the software industry, but has since been adopted across many different endeavours in a wide variety of industries. Leaders are acknowledging the importance of valuing people and culture more highly than the output they produce. Improving output is valuable today, but supporting the growth and learning of people will be valuable long into the future.

Agile is easy to understand but difficult to master.

It is easy to understand the Agile Manifesto; you can quite literally read the whole thing in a couple of minutes. But there are hidden meanings to the values and principles that are not obvious – and only through practice and experience will true understanding emerge.

The Agile Manifesto was born in the software industry, but has evolved and transcended, and is now applied across just about every industry there is. I've seen agile applied with huge benefits in marketing, HR, sales, legal, logistics and many other disciplines.

Agile has also grown beyond the world of work and has become a mindset that can be applicable to all areas of your life. An agile mindset can help you approach any difficulty, task or decision.

Adopting agile is a journey, not a destination or end-goal.

As people, teams and organisations adopt agile, they always start with doing agile practices. Those practices will help you improve the way you conceive, plan, and complete work. The practice will seem strange and uncomfortable to start with, but after following it for a while, the way you think about the work will change and the deeper meaning of the practice will be revealed.

Once the practice has become second-nature, and you've absorbed those deeper meanings, you'll be able to define your own practices, perhaps even changing the basics in ways that make them even more powerful for your context. That is the point are which you have evolved from *doing* agile to *being* agile.

In this section we cover:

- What is Agile?
- A Venn Diagram of Agility
- Purpose
- Flow
- Change
- Learning or Winning
- Growth is not Comfortable
- Making Sense
- Cognitive Biases
- Feedback
- You Can't See the Label From Inside the Jar

CHAPTER 1

What is Agile?

Agile is a mindset and a way of being. It is not a framework – because it doesn't give you a frame within which you do your work. It is not a methodology – because it doesn't give you methods.

Agile is a set of 4 values and 12 principles created to help people see the craft of software development differently. It has evolved beyond software so that it can be applied by any team in any organisation, and it is ready to be further evolved so that it can be relevant to the individual.

People first.

The work people do, the products and services they build, the tools they use and the processes they follow are all valuable, but the people are *more* valuable. An agile individual knows that *people* make everything happen.

More planning.

An agile individual knows that we cannot foresee everything that will happen in any large complex endeavour, and they are comfortable working in an environment where there is a lot of uncertainty. They know that planning is essential even if the plan itself is worthless because too much will change before the work is completed, so they continually revisit their plans all the time.

Change is inevitable so bring about positive change.

Being agile means being OK with change, even change that disrupts your plans. The pace of change in the world is increasing and you cannot foresee every change before it happens. An agile individual isn't just comfortable with change – they work to bring positive change about in the world and in themselves.

Always seek feedback.

Living with an agile mindset means valuing feedback, even if it is not positive, because that is how we can grow and improve. An agile individual actively seeks out feedback and then reflects on how they can use that feedback to learn.

WHAT IS AGILE?

Learning is more valuable than being right.

Learning is more valuable than being right. An agile individual knows that making a point or winning an argument is worthless, because they have not learned anything about themselves or others. Instead, they listen so they can learn. Being right feels good for a moment, but learning is valuable for the rest of your life.

Reflect on performance and be aware of bias.

Being agile means being self-aware, accepting that we are all flawed, and we all have biases. An agile individual is aware of bias, and they regularly reflect on their performance so they can improve.

Make sense of the system.

It is essential for the agile individual to make sense of the human systems in which we operate. They carry many mental models in their toolkit that they apply differently to each situation so they can build a deeper understanding of the relationships within the system and creatively find alternative ways of dealing with things.

Have a compelling purpose and a vision for the long term.

Your ability to be agile is dramatically improved when you have a clear and compelling purpose, and you know where you want to go. Everything from choosing the work you do to deciding priorities and choosing how you go about your work is enhanced when your purpose is clear, and you know where you are going.

Ruthless prioritisation at all levels.

Everything is prioritised: from the really big things that contribute to your purpose down to the smallest tasks that you need to complete today – so you're always working on the most valuable and important things.

Focus with laser like intensity on one thing at a time.

With clarity on their priorities, an agile individual focuses on just one thing at a time and doesn't start another piece of work until the first one is finished. If something can't be finished in one go, it is split into smaller tasks that can be.

Create clarity on problems and opportunities before thinking about solutions.

Being agile involves creating clarity on the problem you are solving or the opportunity you are exposing before investing effort in designing a solution. The agile individual knows that leaping to a solution before fully understanding the problem leads to investing effort in the wrong things.

Work on root causes not symptoms.

Investing effort in understanding root causes is infinitely more valuable than resolving symptoms. Solving a symptom doesn't fix the underlying problem, but fixing the root cause solves it permanently.

Create outcomes not outputs.

An agile individual tries to bring about outcomes, or positive results, with as little output as possible. Output is only valuable if it contributes to outcomes.

Simplicity in all things.

Being agile means making things as simple as possible. Making everything simpler creates opportunities to achieve better outcomes with less effort.

Break large complex outcomes into small tasks.

The smaller and simpler each individual task is, the more likely it is that it can be completed in one go with high quality.

BE AGILE

Incremental improvements created in short iterations.

An agile individual knows that small, incremental improvements that can be completed quickly contribute to the longer-term outcomes better than large improvements that take a long time. They work in short iterations to deliver each incremental improvement.

Make work visible.

Being agile means making work visible so progress can be seen at a glance, bottlenecks in processes become evident and obstacles are quickly eliminated.

Make decisions empirically.

Decisions backed by real data are better than those based on hunches or anecdotes. By carefully measuring every aspect of their practices and processes, an agile individual makes better decisions.

Agile is collaborative.

Working together with those who supply you with inputs and those who will receive your outputs creates powerful value streams that uplift everyone's performance. Understanding the context of those upstream helps you to plan your own work and to help uplift theirs. Understanding the context of those downstream helps you to improve your product or service in ways that actually matter to them.

Activity: How agile am I Worksheet

Use this worksheet to obtain a view of your current agility.

The result is not important and cannot be used to compare your agility to that of another person, what is important is that it gives you visibility of areas of agility you can choose to do something about.

Rate yourself for each area by placing a check mark where you believe you sit between the two statements.

You can download a 'How agile am I worksheet' at https://www.terryhaayema.com/templates

My purpose is clear and compelling				I don't know my purpose
My goals are clearly defined and motivating				I don't have goals
I have plans for achieving my goals				I don't have plans for achieving my goals

My plans are high level for future work				My plans are detailed for future work, (or I don't have plans)
My high-level plans are based on outcomes				My plans are based on something other than outcomes
The outcomes in my high-level plans are prioritised				I know what I want to achieve, but it's not prioritised
I break high level goals into small simple work items				I don't break down high level goals
My plans are detailed for my current work				My work is responsive, 'putting out fires' (or I don't have plans)
I regularly review and adjust my plans				My plans are locked in, (or I don't have plans)
I regularly pause and reflect on how I'm going so I can improve				I don't reflect on how I'm going
I work on one thing at a time so I can focus				I'm always multi-tasking

I use metrics to understand and improve my performance					I don't measure my performance
I try out small things quickly rather than big things perfectly					I stick with something until it is perfect
I am an agent for positive change					I value stability and am uncomfortable with change
I work at a pace I can sustain indefinitely					I'm often working long hours and sometimes feel burnt out
I try to make everything as simple as possible					I do what is asked of me without trying to find a simpler way
I invest in mastering my craft, learning is in everything I do					I don't have time for learning
I value diversity of opinion; I know I can learn from everyone					I prefer to seek the opinions of those like me

CHAPTER 2

A Venn Diagram of Agility

To help understand what agile is, it helps to know that each of the frameworks and methodologies that have sprung up around it have an intent behind their practices that isn't always obvious from the practice itself.

Looking across all the practices and processes from the wide variety of frameworks and methodologies that respect the Agile Manifesto, you find that while there are differences in their processes and practices, there is common ground in their intent. They are all trying to achieve a balance between doing the right thing, doing the thing right and shortening the learning cycle.

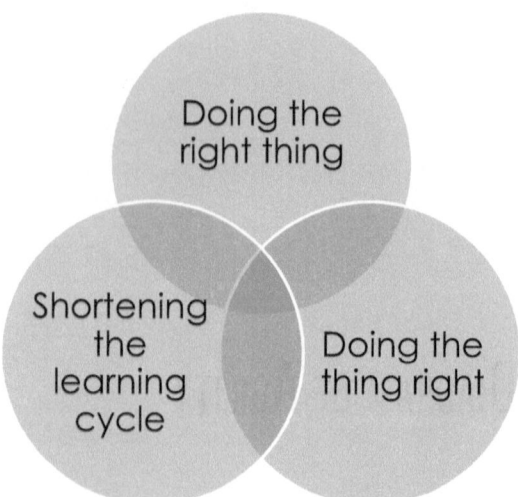

'Doing the right thing' means keeping your eyes on the prize, having a compelling purpose for why we exist as a Team, being crystal clear on our vision for the future, constantly confirming the most valuable thing we should be working on and how it contributes to our vision and assessing what we've done to ensure we're progressing towards meaningful goals.

'Doing the thing right' involves a dedication to quality and doing the very best we can in every task we take on, working to deliver what the customer wants in ways that continue to improve over time.

And 'shortening the learning cycle' describes working in smaller batches so you can learn about what the customer values and how we can get better at delivering it as you go. Rather than waiting until we have something big to give the customer, we work

A VENN DIAGRAM OF AGILITY

incrementally and iteratively, adding small improvements and seeking feedback after each one so we can learn more about what the customer values.

It is incredibly difficult to maintain a balance between the three imperatives, but it is worthwhile.

When you have them in balance, you're delivering the products or services that people want with quality that meets their expectations at a pace that is fast enough.

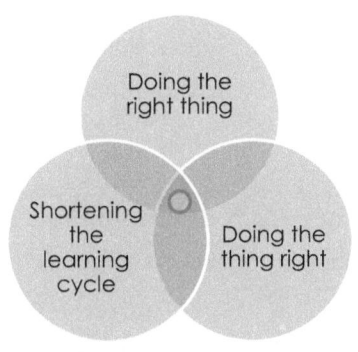

You could represent that on the Venn diagram as a dot, right in the sweet spot in the middle of all three circles.

When the three imperatives are close enough to being in balance, they become self-reinforcing.

Doing the right thing involves always working on what is most valuable for the customer with an acceptance that we cannot have much certainty about the future. Knowing that we can't be sure that something we have worked on for 12 months will still be valuable in 12 months' time requires us to shorten the learning cycle by working in short iterations delivering incremental improvements. It also encourages us to deliver high quality because low quality services or products would definitely not be the right thing for the customer.

Doing the thing right helps us to improve our practices and processes as we work together, allowing us to deliver faster and shorten the learning cycle while also improving our technical capabilities – which opens opportunities to get better at doing the right thing.

Short learning loops help us understand what customers value. We get better at doing the right thing, and build a better relationship with the customer. This, in turn, gives us a greater desire to delivery better quality, and develop an obsession with doing the thing right.

Focusing too much on one of the three means you hamper your chances of success.

If your focus is too far towards doing the right thing, then you could be delivering exactly the product or service that people want, but the quality may be poor and long learning cycles take too long to get it into their hands.

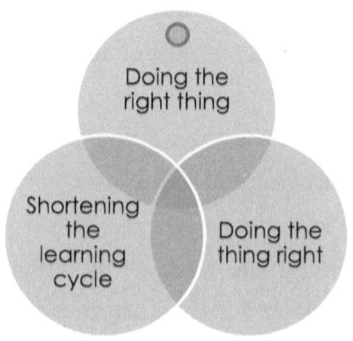

Delivering the right thing is incredibly important, but it has to be balanced with working in short cycles so you quickly learn what the customer really values. Without short learning cycles, how do you know it is the right thing? The customer's needs may have changed while you were developing a solution.

A VENN DIAGRAM OF AGILITY

Delivering the right thing must also be balanced with doing the thing right. If your product matches exactly what the customer wants, but the quality doesn't meet their standards, it isn't really the right thing anymore and they are more likely to abandon it.

If your focus is too far towards doing the thing right, then you could be delivering something that is very high quality, but it isn't what people want and long learning cycles result in taking too long to get it to them.

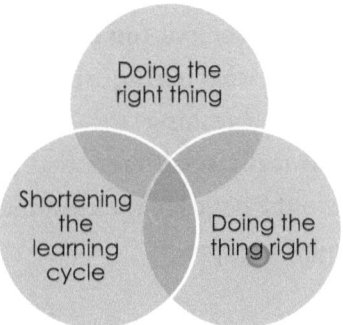

Delivering high quality products or services is essential but focusing too much on this imperative at the expense of the other 2 results in 'gold plating' that ends up delivering something of a higher quality than people want at the expense of meeting their actual needs and delivering at speed.

Some areas of your product or service will need to have absolutely the highest quality possible. These non-negotiable areas must still be delivered properly, or you create even bigger problems for your customers and for yourself. If you're making teddy bears for example, there can be no compromise in the quality of how the eyes are attached, or you could create a product that is dangerous for children.

Every product has some non-negotiable areas of quality, but they also have areas where it is possible to go too far and reduce your ability to keep the three imperatives in balance. In the teddy bear example, you could end up 'gold plating' the quality by stuffing the teddy with materials of a higher quality than necessary or lining the packaging with silk and delivering qualities that your customer doesn't value or doesn't even notice.

What if you put **too much emphasis on shortening the learning cycles**, breaking the work down into really small tasks that you get into the hands of the customer with lightning speed?

It is arguable that shortening the learning cycles will provide feedback sooner so you can adjust and get better at understanding what the customer values, but on its own, a focus on short learning cycles will still lead to problems.

Neglecting even one of the three imperatives will leave you with difficulties in delivering what your customers want.

What if your attention was taken up with doing the right thing AND doing the thing right but you were neglecting shortening the learning cycle?

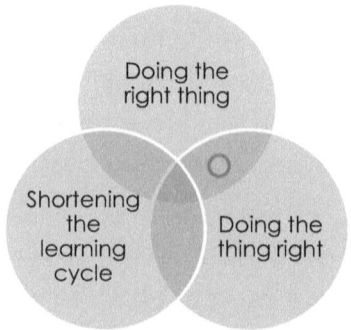

A VENN DIAGRAM OF AGILITY

This would be creating a teddy bear that exactly meets what people want at the highest possible quality but taking a long time to do it.

Without enough energy given to shortening the learning cycle, it would take you a long time to get anything into the hands of your customers and your feedback would be delayed, making it hard for you to learn more about what the customer values.

You'd be making good quality teddy bears that your customers want to buy, but they'd be taking too long to make and any changes in customer desires or moves by your competitors would be missed.

What if you were focused on short learning cycles AND doing the right thing without much attention being paid to the quality of your product?

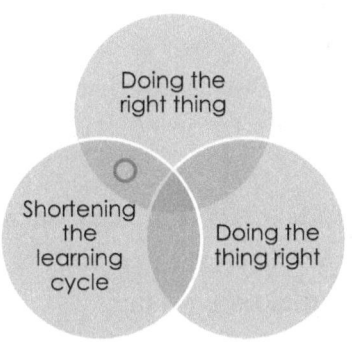

Creating the teddy bear customers want and doing it quickly, but with questionable quality.

With insufficient investment in quality, your product might do well in the marketplace for a short time, but eventually the cost of dealing with defects and the rate at which customers abandon your brand would mount up.

You'd be delivering what the customer wants and doing it quickly, but customers would likely become disillusioned with your product due to an unacceptable level of defects.

Imagine you were building a product of exceptional quality AND delivering it in short cycles so you were learning quickly, but didn't have an eye on what the customer really wants.

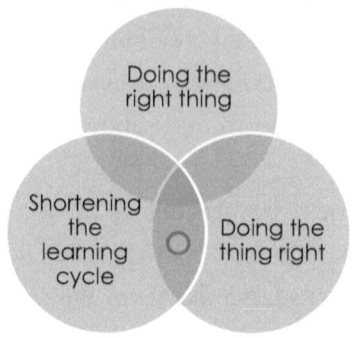

Your teddy bear would be one of the best-quality teddy bears available and it would be quick to get to market – but without the features or design that customers are looking for, it may not sell well at all.

Without enough focus on what customers really want, you can invest in creating products or services that simply don't match what your customer wants.

Doing the right thing doesn't always mean doing exactly what customers are asking for. Sometimes you have a better understanding of the problems your customer is dealing with than they do themselves – and the right thing might be something they would never think to ask for. The iPhone is a good example of doing the right thing, even though no one knew to ask for it. Until we had one in our hands, we would never have thought to request a phone without any buttons.

The ideal then, is to try to find that sweet spot right in the middle, between having what customers want while also ensuring that your quality always exceeds the customers' expectations with a solid dedication to the non-negotiables – and still ensuring that you're working in short iterations with frequent and regular learning.

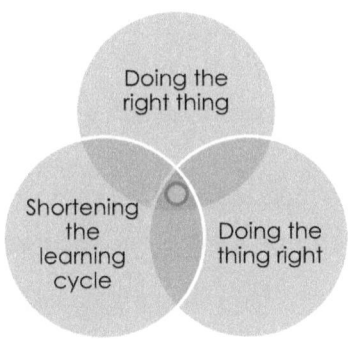

There is no suggestion that this is simple or easy. In fact, it is immensely difficult! But it is worthwhile and will pay you back many times over. You will find your work drifting from the sweet spot most of the time and will likely have to adjust one thing or another. But keep at it! In any complex endeavour, this will require constant attention.

Activity

Assess the work you're doing in relation to the product or service you provide to your customers, and identify where it fits on the Venn diagram. Is there too much focus on one or two of the three imperatives? Or are you close enough to the centre and only small adjustments are necessary?

Thinking about each of the three imperatives, distribute 10 points across them to show how much of your focus goes to each one. For example, if most of your focus is on quality with a roughly even split across the other two, you might give 'Doing the thing right' 8 points and the others 1 point each.

You can download the 'Venn diagram of agile worksheet' at https://www.terryhaayema.com/templates

	Doing the right thing	Doing the thing right	Short learning cycles
Points			

Draw a dot where your efforts are directed in the product or service you deliver for each of the three imperatives, then join the dots to form a triangle and position your final dot in the middle of that triangle.

In the example above you would have something like this:

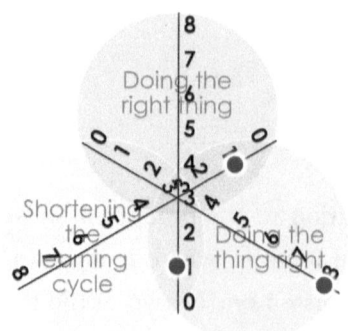

Step 1: Draw a dot where your focus is for each of the three imperatives.

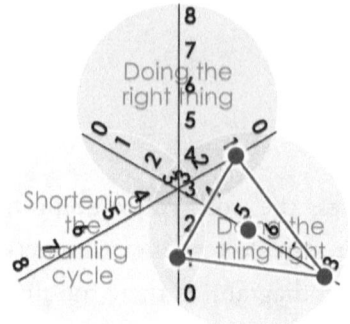

Step 2: Join the dots to form a triangle and place the final dot in the centre.

A VENN DIAGRAM OF AGILITY

Now draw your dots, form your triangle and place your focal point for the 3 imperatives.

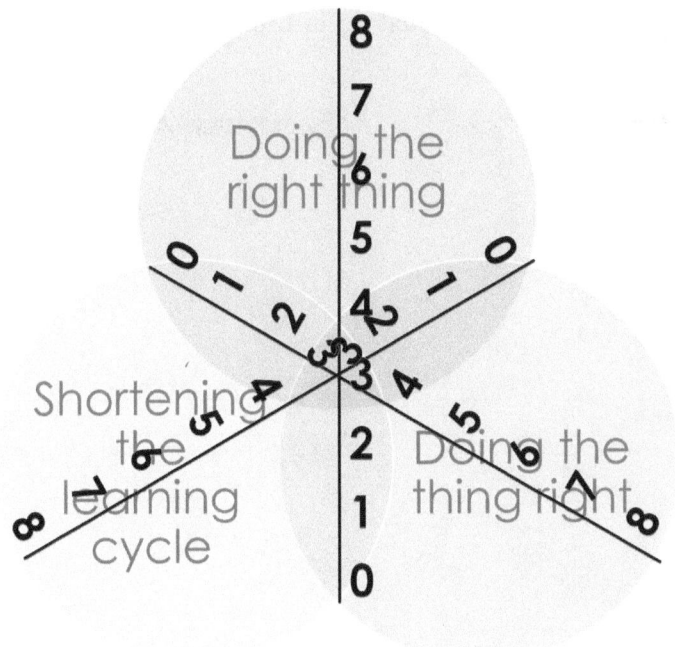

Don't feel discouraged if your dot falls somewhere outside the centre of the diagram. This is quite likely the first time you've thought about your work this way.

Be grateful that you now have visibility of a possible imbalance and a way to assess it any time you want to assess your balance of the three imperatives.

Having that visibility is enormously valuable, because now you can choose to do something about it.

What is one thing you could do to bring the focus closer to the centre?

Current focus	One thing I could do differently

CHAPTER 3

Purple

What is your personal purpose? Why are you here?

Having a personal purpose is a powerful tool in helping you to choose what you must learn, what you want to work on and how you will go about it.

When I first came across the idea of having a personal purpose, I reflected deeply on what my purpose should be. I considered my strengths and capabilities and the work that I enjoyed most and arrived at a purpose statement that felt like it fit me perfectly.

"Helping organisations develop agility"

This was immensely helpful at the time in directing my learning toward organisational agility, psychology and leadership. My personal purpose statement directed me towards work that allowed me to express my 'why' and add a lot of value for the people around me.

My work evolved over time and I started taking on bigger, more complex coaching engagements in larger, more corporate organisations. The constraints were mounting along with the politics, and while I was loving every minute of the work with people, I was becoming more and more dissatisfied with the nature of the organisations and the prevailing top-down command and control cultures I encountered.

After a few years of working through this purpose statement, my dissatisfaction mounted to the point where I realised: I didn't actually care about organisations developing agility at all!

My real passion was helping the *people* in those organisations, not the organisation itself. Organisational agility was an aspect of my work, but it was no longer serving me as a purpose.

Once again, I stepped back into self-reflection to see if I could reform my 'why' into something that resonated more closely with who I am and why I get out of bed in the morning.

After several weeks allowing various formulations to spin around in my sub-conscious, I arrived at my new and improved personal purpose:

> *"Helping people find the joy in work"*

This purpose statement fit me much better. It aligned to my character, the things I enjoyed working on and the learning I found most interesting.

Over the next few years, I worked with this purpose statement and found it to be remarkably valuable in maintaining a focus on people and helping them to find joy. It gave me immense joy and satisfaction to see the look on people's faces when a new concept came to life for them in ways that helped them discover joy in their work.

But once again, dissatisfaction started to creep in. Helping people find joy was spot on, it's the reason I get out of bed in the morning, but I realised I don't care so much about work.

At around that time, I came across a wonderful book called "Find Your Why" by Simon Sinek, David Mead and Peter Docker. This book proposes working with someone you trust to coach you through of finding your purpose by focusing on the impact and contribution you have made or that you want to make on the people around you.

Collaborating with Amanda Clarke, a wonderful Agile Coach I worked with at the Commonwealth Bank of Australia, we coached each other through the process to arrive at our new purpose statements.

My new and improved purpose statement, created through this facilitated coaching process became:

"Helping people see differently so they find joy"

This remains my purpose statement to this day and has proven to be the most powerful one yet.

Everything is better when work is joyful! My mission is no longer to make that work joyful, but to help people to see it differently. Helping people to find other ways to solve problems, find opportunities, or simplify solutions are all part of it, but the focus now is on helping people to see things differently not on the work itself.

Two years later, and I am still using my 'why' to direct my learning, choose the projects to work on and decide how to go about the work. So far there has been no dissatisfaction with any part of it and it is growing ever more powerful and effective in helping me evolve and grow.

Having this as my purpose helps me to feel more connected to my work and gives me much more meaningful ways in which to measure outcomes. In fact, it is the reason I'm writing this very book.

If you don't have a clearly-defined purpose, then create one. Even if your first draft is something you create through self-reflection, it will be a significant benefit in bringing joy to your work and your learning. If you have access to a trusted coach, then consider following the facilitated approach for a more impactful personal purpose.

Activity

What is your why?

Define your personal purpose statement.

If you can get your hands on a copy of, "Find Your Why," by Simon Sinek, David Mead and Peter Docker, read it and collaborate with someone you trust to facilitate each other's purpose statement. This will be a fantastic experience and is well worth the time investment.

If not, reflect on why you get out of bed in the morning. What is it about your work that you are passionate about? Reflect on your previous jobs or the time you were at school or university. What amongst your past successes gives you pride?

For me, the initial journey towards my first purpose statement was through considering my strengths and abilities and the work I enjoyed most. For you, it might be the things you're good at in your work, or it might be about the things you do with your family or in the community. What is it that you do with those strengths?

When you have clarity on your strengths and abilities, think about why you use those strengths. What outcomes do your strengths create for people or communities?

Then put it together using the, "<something you do> so that <some outcome>" format.

My Personal Purpose	
Something I do	The outcome of doing it
so that	

CHAPTER 4

FLOW

Flow is a concept from positive psychology first identified by Mihály Csíkszentmihályi in 1975 that can be described as, 'being in the zone.'

Some people might find it counter intuitive to connect the idea of flow with anything to do with being agile. At a team and organisational level, there are a lot of agile concepts and practices that support improving the flow of valuable customer outcomes through a team or groups of teams. If you want to be more a more agile individual, then flow is the same thing for you, when you are in a state flow, the quality and quantity of the outcomes you produce will also improve, along with your creativity and ability to innovate.

Flow is the mental state in which you become so fully immersed in an activity that you enter a feeling of absolute focus. Your entire being is absorbed by the activity and you completely lose track of time.

In a state of flow, you become so engaged in the activity that your mind and body become one and you no longer need to think about individual actions.

> *FIND A JOB YOU ENJOY DOING, AND YOU WILL NEVER HAVE TO WORK A DAY IN YOUR LIFE.*
> Mark Twain

You are completely present with the activity and no distraction can interrupt you. You operate with immense energy, creativity blossoms and the quality of what you produce is significantly higher than what you could normally create.

During a flow state, concepts emerge as if from nowhere, and you feel as if you are channelling some higher life force with creative ideas emerging so fluidly that you can't remember how they arose or where they came from.

The flow state most often arises when multiple aspects of an activity come together to create a state of being fully present with the task.

Some of these factors may be:

- You enjoy the activity
- It is intrinsically motivating
- You are reasonably good at it
- You are in control of the situation or activity
- There is a clear goal
- You have a good chance to succeed with it

- The activity is difficult enough to be challenging, but not so difficult as to create anxiety
- You give it your complete attention, eliminating all distractions

As you can readily see from the list above, the closer you are to proficiency in an activity, the more likely it is to put you into a state of flow.

But how do you reach a flow state?

There are 2 main elements to achieving a state of flow:

- What you choose to work on
- How you go about the work

Choosing the work that enables a flow state

When you choose work that enables you to achieve that state of flow, you not only create a space within which you can achieve a great deal of joy and satisfaction, but you also enable a space where the quality and quantity of your output is exponentially increased.

Don't worry for the moment whether it can provide you with the income you need or whether it is considered a worthy occupation by others. The key is to find something you enjoy doing. It might start out as a hobby or pastime, but if you love it, you will give it more energy, more passion and you'll stick with it for longer.

If you love an activity, you will find ways to learn about it. Mentors will appear serendipitously to help you grow because your subconscious will be looking for things that match the patterns of reward that it gives you. With such a compelling activity, you will be more likely to persevere when things are difficult, or you're obstructed.

When you love an activity, you will engage with communities of like-minded people who also enjoy that activity – and through that you'll learn even more and grow further. Growing your profile within that community will happen because you are one of the people with enough passion for it to go beyond the investment most people make, you'll do the activity harder than others and for longer than others.

Just about any activity can be transformed into a lucrative career when you have developed yourself into a master in the field.

Case study: Hedgehog Hollow

Alexandra Stapleton-Smith was leading a successful career as Globalization Business Development Manager at Jaguar Cars when she became very ill after the birth of her second child. After the family moved from the UK to USA and unable to get a work visa, Alexandra needed something to fill in time and turned to her passion for arts and crafts, starting an arts and crafts blog and YouTube channel she named "Hedgehog Hollow,"

The joy Alexandra found in making things with her hands, carried over into the creation of her blog. And the challenge and learning from taking her passion into a completely new area created the flow state that allowed her to persist through the difficulties and learn from the mistakes without being discouraged.

Today, Hedgehog Hollow has over 100,000 subscribers across YouTube, Instagram, Facebook and Pintrest. Alexandra's hobby has turned into a successful online retailer of craft materials where people can subscribe to monthly deliveries of craft projects along with all the materials needed to complete them.

What are you passionate about? Is there a hobby that you love that you find yourself slipping into a state of flow? Maybe you could turn that hobby into a side hustle or even a lucrative business.

Going about the work in a way that enables a flow state

Having identified an activity that you love, you should go about it with intensity, invest yourself into it, and give it everything you've got.

If you are finding it too challenging, try taking it on in smaller chunks. Tasks that are too challenging might lead to frustration and anxiety, but often that frustration transforms into flow if you can approach it one small step at a time.

On the other hand, if you discover the task is not challenging your abilities, then there won't be much learning to take from it and you probably won't experience the flow state. Tasks that are not challenging enough can lead to boredom and complacency. How can you give it a little spice to add a little challenge? Can you approach it in a new way? Or include an additional element? What is the next step in how this work or activity might evolve?

Don't seek to make your chosen tasks too easy or too difficult, just challenging enough to fully engage you in solving the problems and overcoming the difficulties.

Self-awareness as you go about the work is particularly important. Maintain an internal barometer of enjoyment. If you're enjoying the task, you are more likely to enter the flow state, if you aren't enjoying it, what can you do differently to make it more joyful?

To make a task more fun, try a few of these ideas:

- Approach it from another angle. Try looking at the task from the point of view of making it fun
- Separate the output from the task. Sometimes stressing about the quality or quantity of output eliminates the fun in doing the task. A task can be more intrinsically motivating when you don't have to worry about the end game
- Add music, either in the background or singing along
- Change the setting. Brighter surroundings might inject a little fun

- Do it with other people. A task that is not so much fun when you are doing it alone can become immensely enjoyable when you do it together with other people
- Get creative! Allow yourself to inject humour or wit into the task

Eliminate distractions in the task, in yourself and in your surroundings. A **distraction** is anything that reduces your ability to have **traction**.

- Turn off email notifications
- Put your phone on flight mode or turn it off all together
- Avoid the temptation to check social media
- Put on noise-cancelling headphones to eliminate distracting noise
- Get away from other people if they are likely to want to talk to you
- Organise your workspace. Remove anything that isn't necessary for the task and ensure the tools you need are close at hand

Your email and social media will still be there when you are finished and can be dealt with at that point. Allowing them to grab your attention whenever a notification arrives puts you in a constant state of distraction and will make it next to impossible to operate with flow. Choosing a time to deal with them that suits you and giving yourself a nice block of time for deep traction with the task maximises your opportunity to experience flow.

Being in a state of flow allows you to bring more creativity to solving problems, it allows you to be more adaptable when difficulties arise, and – overall – helps you to be more agile in your mindset.

Activity

Identify your flow state activities.

Flow state can be a tricky thing to identify, but with patience and time you can figure it out.

You can download a Find Your Flow worksheet at https://www.terryhaayema.com/templates

Step 1: reflect on the things you love to do.

What activities completely captivate you, that are just challenging enough to consume your entire attention, and you're good enough at them to get quality results most of the time? They make time fly, and you lose track of what's happening around you.

As you reflect on each activity, give it a score out of 10, and write down the activities that score 8 or more.

Things I love to do	Flow Score

Step 2: come up with some ways you can bring more of the activities you love into your life.

Think about each of the activities that scored the highest flow scores.

Don't limit your thinking to just doing more of each activity. Instead, go broad: consider ways you can incorporate them into other areas of your life. Can you approach your work in a way that allows you to build in the activities you love? Maybe you can write about your passion, or create a YouTube channel. Is there a community based around your flow activity? If not could you start one?

Flow activity	Ways I might bring more if it into my life

CHAPTER 5

CHANGE

An agile individual is comfortable with change.

More than being comfortable with change, an agile individual knows that change is inevitable and fully expects change to come from every direction all the time.

> THERE IS NOTHING PERMANENT EXCEPT CHANGE.
> *Heraclitus*

The second principle in the agile manifesto states that, "Agile processes harness change for the customer's competitive advantage." Not only does the agile individual expect change with an acceptance that it is inevitable, they also harness that change as a force for good in their service of their customers.

More even than expecting change and harnessing it for the good of those they serve, the agile individual creates change, being an agent of change in everything they do.

Being comfortable with change and knowing change will come no matter what we do, the agile individual focuses their attention on bringing change for good. They create a constant stream of small improvements in their practices, processes, behaviours and thinking.

Most people are driven by the desire for comfort. This is normal, it is human, and it is a survival instinct that has served us well.

> LOOK UP AT THE STARS AND NOT DOWN AT YOUR FEET. TRY TO MAKE SENSE OF WHAT YOU SEE, AND WONDER ABOUT WHAT MAKES THE UNIVERSE EXIST. BE CURIOUS.
> Stephen Hawking

Being in a dangerous situation is inherently uncomfortable, so the subconscious drives a mindset for seeking comfort in order to keep us safe.

However, the subconscious does not know the difference between the stress of a life-threatening predator or the stress of being outside our comfort zone, so it responds in the same way to either threat. While it makes perfect sense to avoid dangerous beasts, it does not make sense to avoid change in an ever-changing world, even if that change isn't immediately comfortable.

The world is ever-changing, and nothing stays the same for long. If you're not keeping ahead of the changes, then you're falling behind. There is no staying still when everything around you is changing.

As an individual with an agile mindset, you take it a step further: it is not enough to keep up with external changes. Instead, you become an agent for change. This way, you take agency over your own destiny to help bring about change for good, rather than change for change's sake.

Beyond being able to influence change rather than being influenced by it, change brings learning opportunities and those learning opportunities are fantastic vehicles for personal growth.

Case Study: The Dream Team

A notable example of bringing change for good is a team I worked with several years ago.

The team was having difficulty finishing anything because their requirements kept changing while they were working on things. Even after they finished something the requirements would change again before they could secure sign off.

In response to their ever-changing requirements, they invested enormous effort in analysis and documenting what was needed. The difficulty with their approach is that they had multiple stakeholders who all wanted something different, and they weren't talking to each other.

Whenever they got clarity from one stakeholder on what was required, another stakeholder would complain that it didn't fit their business model and had to be done differently.

Another contributing cause to the problem is that people can't imagine what the result will be when they ask for something. Even with excruciatingly detailed documentation, what the person asking for something is imagining will be different in some way to what the team will build. Showing their stakeholders what was built after it was finished always resulted in something emerging that needed to be done differently.

The team felt like they were the victims of change inflicted upon them by stakeholders who had no understanding of the complexity or difficulty of what they were asking for. Instead of being the victims of change, the team decided that they would become the instigators of change.

The change the team implemented was to stop documenting what was required up front and start documenting what was built as they went along. This involved establishing a planning and delivery governance forum that included all of their stakeholders in a 15-minute meeting twice a week with longer sessions when necessary.

Instead of spending all their time running from one stakeholder to another to create ever more detailed documents, they convened a longer session of the stakeholder forum when they started a new piece of work in which the stakeholders themselves could figure out what was needed between them. Each stakeholder gained an understanding of the context of the other stakeholders, and they became much more flexible in what they demanded.

At the shorter bi-weekly sessions, the team would demonstrate what they were working on, even if it was nowhere near complete. This helped the stakeholders to imagine what the result would be because they could see it emerging and give feedback on it before the team went too far down the wrong path. When the feedback was that something was wrong, it emerged in front of all the other stakeholders so all the inputs to a change could be discussed and all views considered before it was taken on, eliminating the need to go back and forth between stakeholders and get only a small piece of the puzzle from each one.

The outcome of replacing documentation with conversation was that the team went from several months to deliver something to just a week or two. Not only did the pace of their delivery increase, but the quality improved as well.

Stakeholders were delighted, they felt that they were being listened to and that their input was valuable. Their impression of the team went from one that was slow and expensive to one that understood their needs better and delivered great work.

The team were ecstatic, no longer were they spending time on work that felt unimportant and they developed a sense of achievement with a feeling that they were valued.

BE AGILE

Activity

Bringing change for good.

What is one thing you will change? Something you will take ownership of and create a change rather than waiting for change to come from elsewhere.

Like the Dream Team, look for something in your work that is causing you difficulty and turn it into something that creates joy by making a small change in the way you approach it.

Think about the way your work progresses from being an idea to being something that is complete, what are the points along that flow of work that cause delays, rework or add complexity.

When you've selected the thing you want to change, try to identify the contributing factors that make it a difficulty. In the case of the Dream Team, the problem seemed to be that their requirements kept changing, but the contributing factors were about how they engaged with their stakeholders, they tried changing the level of detail in their requirements, but that didn't work. Engaging more closely and more often with their stakeholders was the change that made the difference.

With clarity on what needs to change and the factors that contribute to it, get creative about what you will do to change it.

- What happens if you stop doing it all together?
- What is the impact of doing the exact opposite?
- Can someone else do it?
- Are there relationships that need to improve?
- Is there a simpler way to approach it?

Adaptability

Adaptability is the ability of an organism to adapt to different environments. A plant or animal can be said to be adaptable when it can cope with a wide range of different circumstances. Humans are said to be the most adaptable creatures on our planet because we can live in just about every environment on the planet, even if we have to use technology to do so.

From the point of view of personal agility, adaptability relates to your ability to succeed in different environments, cultures, systems, etc.

> *INTELLIGENCE IS THE ABILITY TO ADAPT TO CHANGE.*
> Stephen Hawking

Being successful in a given system is wonderful, but every system changes over time. Entropy dictates that every system left to its own devices will gradually decline into disorder.

The adaptability of a person or system is their ability and/or willingness to change in response to changing circumstances and to quickly learn new skills and develop new capabilities in response to changes around them.

Adaptability requires flexibility, especially when things don't go to plan. It requires a willingness to try a different approach to what we have always done – because what we have done in the past will not necessarily serve us in the future.

Most jobs today involve dealing with unexpected circumstances. The adaptable person can deal with the unexpected without needing to receive explicit instructions from their leaders. They can think on their feet, make decisions, solve problems, and realise opportunities without needing to ask what to do next.

The less adaptable person might need to ask what to do, waiting for directions from someone in authority. In the accelerated environments we face today, with change occurring faster than ever, that delay may be enough to magnify the impact of a problem or diminish the return on an opportunity. The less adaptable person is much less valuable to their organisation.

In 2019, recruitment company Michael Page published their top 100 most in-demand skills for career success across a wide range of industries based on their assessment of job applicants, job offers and conversations with decision makers. The number one skill they identified for career success was: adaptability.

As your career develops and you grow from *doing* a thing to *managing* it and eventually to *leading* it, the need for adaptability grows as well.

When you are doing the work, you'll need to adapt to what arises relating to the work itself. Hidden complexities and unexpected difficulties will emerge in the process, product or service, requiring you to think on your feet to solve problems and keep the work moving along.

When you are managing the work, soft skills become more important. Empathy, compassion, and trust are vital as you

> IT IS NOT NECESSARY TO CHANGE.
> SURVIVAL IS NOT MANDATORY.
> W. Edwards Deming

are supporting the people who do the work rather than doing the work yourself. The breadth of your scope increases as you now need visibility across the work of all the people in your charge and the system you are managing is much larger than the scope of an individual worker. Managing people is significantly more complex than doing the work. You need to step back a little from the work itself, even though you probably got promoted because you are one of the best at doing it.

When you grow into a leadership role, your scope increases again. You need even more care and trust because there are too many people in your care for you to make all their decisions for them. That would slow everything down and disempower them. Vision, strategy, and influence become key skills in leadership roles, along with networking, empowerment, and delegation.

Developing your adaptability

But how do you develop adaptability? If you accept the importance and value of being adaptable, what can you do to improve your adaptability?

Being okay with being wrong is one of the most important attributes to cultivate if you want to develop adaptability.

When we look back on history, we can't believe some of the things that people held to be true. People used to believe that the world was flat, that sneezing was a sign of being possessed by the devil and that adding formaldehyde to milk would keep it from going off. We know now that those things are not true, but what are the things we hold today to be true that will turn out to be completely wrong in the future?

CHANGE

Holding on to something because we believe it to be true – even in the face of contradictory evidence – stops us from growing and eliminates opportunities to be adaptable.

If we question everything and are okay with some of our most dearly-held beliefs turning out to be incorrect, then we are halfway there to being adaptable.

> THINGS ALWAYS TURN OUT BEST FOR THOSE THAT MAKE THE BEST OUT OF THE WAY THINGS TURN OUT.
> John Wooden

Accepting that anything we think might be wrong allows us to question, check the basis for our beliefs, and be ready to try something different if some piece of evidence contradicts what we previously thought to be true.

But there is a balance in all things. If we accept that what we believe to be true might not be, we are not necessarily stuck in a place where we don't know what to do because we might turn out to be wrong. Being adaptable doesn't mean we get frozen in a cycle of questioning everything; we still need to act.

The key to achieving that balance is confidence that we are acting on the best information available while still being open to our ideas being challenged.

Knowing that we are doing the best we can with the knowledge, skills, abilities and information available should give us the confidence to achieve a balance between that self-belief and the self-awareness to be always observing our own actions, behaviours, beliefs and intentions.

Another technique for developing your adaptability is to put emphasis on *improving* over *proving*.

When you are proving, you are striving at something with a need to demonstrate your capability at it. If whatever you're striving at turns out to be something less than wonderful, it can feel like your capability is questionable. This keeps you driving towards your pre-defined output and makes it harder to pivot if new information arises or you learn something that suggests another approach.

When you're improving, then you're happy to take something on without it being a trophy to your capability. If it doesn't turn out all that well, you can still reflect on what happened and gain learnings from it so you can improve. If the focus is on improving, then new information or learning is readily accepted, and you can adapt your approach.

With a desire to develop your adaptability, you start to become aware of your awareness. Without sounding too meta, it is incredibly valuable in helping you to identify those crucial times when an opportunity to adapt your processes, behaviours or approaches to things arises.

The vast majority of the time, we are not aware of our awareness. We are focused on the work at hand or allowing our minds to think the thoughts that arise in the situation. Every once in a while, pausing to think about your awareness helps you to put

> YOU MUST BE THE CHANGE YOU WISH TO SEE IN THE WORLD.
> Mahatma Gandhi

your thoughts onto a creative track that can spontaneously bring ideas for how to adapt.

Meditation is the single most powerful tool for becoming aware of your awareness. Through meditation, you take a pause from thinking about the task at hand or allowing your mind to wander wherever it wants, to create a pause. In that pause you can consciously choose what to fill it with.

Activity

Write down some of the things that you hold to be true.

What would it mean for you if it turned out they are not true?

Constantly evaluating our strongest-held beliefs helps us to develop the muscle of being adaptable.

Start with the beliefs you hold that are more obviously open to challenge. When you've practiced this for a while you'll find it becomes natural to challenge even closely held beliefs until eventually you can challenge everything.

Consider every step in the work that you do, what do you believe is necessary to complete that step as quickly as possible with high quality? Yours will be unique to your individual context, but you'll create a list of beliefs about the work you perform.

- We need to have detailed plans before we start something.
- I can't test something until after it is built.
- We must finish before the deadline.
- I need to estimate how long something will take.
- I can't demonstrate what I'm working on until it is complete.

Next, consider what it would mean for you if that belief turned out to be incorrect. It doesn't matter at this stage what you need to do to improve the situation, you're just identifying beliefs and considering the implications if those beliefs are challenged.

Things I believe are true	What it would mean if they are not true

CHAPTER 6

Learning or Winning

When things are not going so well, you will have fabulous opportunities to learn, grow and gain experience. When things *are* going well, there are opportunities to achieve results, succeed and to win. Most situations are a blend of the two.

When you react emotionally to your immediate situation without first taking a step back to see the bigger picture, winning seems like a good thing and you will naturally want more of it. Difficulty seems undesirable and you will naturally seek to avoid it, even if you are not consciously doing so.

At times in your life, you will absolutely experience difficulty. At these times, there are more learning opportunities, and success may be nothing more than overcoming the current difficulty. If you let the difficulty overwhelm you, you may miss out on the very learning opportunities that would allow you to gain the experience to contribute to your next success.

Early in my coaching career, I was working under contract with a major financial organisation. My contract was nearing the end of its term and there was a strong commitment by my employer to renew the contract. Every time we discussed it, they made comments about being very happy with my performance and that they were definitely going to renew the contract. The final date was drawing near and still the contract was not renewed. I was following up every day and told it was just waiting for something in the approval chain.

The last day of the contract passed without it being renewed – and suddenly I was out of work. It turns out that the funding for the role was not approved, and the person providing that approval was someone who had no visibility of my performance and with whom I had never interacted.

I didn't succeed at renewing the contract and I didn't overcome the obstacle, even though I had done a good job and could demonstrate that I had exceeded expectations for the role.

Rather than focusing on the difficulty and allowing it to bring me down, I reflected on the learning and discovered some learnings that were far more valuable than the short time I ended up being out of work.

LEARNING OR WINNING

I learned that even if people are telling you everything is proceeding, it may not be in their hands. I learned that your performance may not be the determining factor in whether your contract will be renewed, I also learned that if you don't have a signed renewal in your hand, you need a plan B. And even if people say they will renew it, you need to start looking for the next role a month before the end of the current one, just in case.

Those things I learned from going through that difficulty have helped me to increase the chances of being renewed, and to be ready if it doesn't. I haven't had a single day without work since then.

When you conclude some project successfully, you often experience more feelings of success than learning opportunities. If you allow the feeling of success to dominate your thinking, you may miss the chance to reflect on the journey, the challenges you overcame and the obstacles you created for yourself. Without that reflection, your current success – while enjoyable – will not provide the seeds of learning that lead to even greater success.

> TRY TO LEARN SOMETHING ABOUT EVERYTHING AND EVERYTHING ABOUT SOMETHING.
> Thomas Huxley

Take a broader perspective to any situation, and you will see that winning and difficulty are inextricably intertwined. Overcoming your present difficulty will provide learning that leads to your next success, and examining your present success with a more balanced view will expose areas that could still be improved so you can extract opportunities to grow.

That broader perspective will help you to avoid becoming disheartened in the midst of difficulty because you will find that there is always a learning opportunity to be had.

In the industrial age mindset, we learn everything we need to learn at the beginning of our career and then spend the rest of our life using that knowledge to win at life. With an agile mindset on the other hand, every difficulty along the way is an opportunity to learn and grow, while every outcome, be it a success or a failure is an opportunity to reflect, learn and grow.

Often the learning we gain from overcoming a difficulty is not about the difficulty itself, but something deeper and more personal that appears a long time afterwards – and is only available through self-reflection and an observation of how we've changed and grown as a result.

While in the midst of the difficulty itself, we would wish for that difficulty to simply go away, with the benefit of hindsight, people will often say they are glad they went through the experience because it made them the person they are today.

LEARNING OR WINNING

Activity

Learning or winning – change your viewpoint to change your outcomes.

What big things are you working on?

What does it mean to you if you succeed at them? What does it mean if you don't succeed?

What would the impact be if you were to redefine those big achievements into learning opportunities?

Do it now.

Big thing I'm working on	Redefined as a learning opportunity

Now you can approach how you go about the work differently. Regardless of whether you succeed or not, you will learn along the way. That learning may well turn out to be more valuable in the long run than the outcome itself.

What is causing you difficulty?

What does it mean to you if the difficulty results in a negative outcome? What does it mean if it turns out positively?

How would it change the way you see the difficulty if you were to redefine it as an opportunity to learn?

Do it now.

Something I'm struggling with	Redefined as a learning opportunity

CHAPTER 7

Growth is Not Comfortable

An agile individual knows that staying within their comfort zone hampers their opportunities to gain experience, learn and grow.

Knowing when you are in your comfort zone isn't always obvious, however – and even with personal reflection, it can be difficult to see the boundaries of your comfort zone.

> THE CAVE YOU FEAR TO ENTER HOLDS THE TREASURES THAT YOU SEEK
> Joseph Campbell

So how do you know when you're in your comfort zone or when you're avoiding the things that might take you outside of it?

One simple way to identify where your comfort zone is, and whether you're dodging opportunities to go beyond it, is to reflect on the things that you're not doing. What are you procrastinating about? What are you skilfully avoiding? What have you been putting off?

The things you're avoiding might just be boring or meaningless to you. I know I procrastinate about all sorts of administrative tasks – that doesn't mean they will take me outside my comfort zone and offer areas for growth, it just means I don't like them.

We're looking for the things you're avoiding because they are uncomfortable. Maybe you're putting off a difficult conversation, or delaying getting started on a challenging task, or avoiding taking something on because you it might make you look less than awesome. Whatever it is for you, once you've identified it, then it's time to get started.

Don't take giant leaps into the uncomfortable. It's important not to get too caught up with the idea of escaping your comfort zone. Any endeavour that is too far outside your comfort zone has the potential to create anxiety or become dangerous. You're looking for that sweet spot where you are far enough outside your comfort zone that you are experiencing challenge but not so far outside it that you feel out of your depth.

When venturing into the uncomfortable, seek out opportunities to grow and learn that don't require you to be all the way there. If you're putting off a difficult project because you've never done that sort of thing before, there might be a meetup you can join or someone in your network who has experience in that area and is happy to share how they go about it.

When you've chosen an area to explore that you feel will take you beyond what you've done before and be challenging enough to get

GROWTH IS NOT COMFORTABLE

you outside your comfort zone, break it down. Just like all our work, an agile individual breaks down large or complex things into smaller simpler things that can be prioritised and evaluated with a learning loop in place.

Let's say you've chosen to work on public speaking. This is a brand-new area for you and something you've wanted to do for a long time, but you've never had the courage to take it on. Throwing yourself in front of a large audience to talk about an unfamiliar topic could lead to a very unpleasant experience that breaks your resolve to develop further in this area.

Breaking it down into smaller, less confronting pieces allows you to grow towards your goal and insert opportunities to pause, reflect, grow and plan for the next piece.

In the public speaking example, you might start by joining Toast Masters. At Toast Masters gatherings you can practice speaking in front of a

> *IN ANY GIVEN MOMENT WE HAVE TWO OPTIONS: TO STEP FORWARD INTO GROWTH OR TO STEP BACK INTO SAFETY.*
> Abraham Maslow

group with very short simple exercises that cover both prepared and impromptu speeches. Other attendees are all going through the same journey and know what it's like to be starting out, so they're very supportive and it's a very safe place if you should make a mess of it.

If even Toast Masters is a stretch for you, consider speaking in front of a small group in a virtual setting. That way, it doesn't feel like you're 'in front' of people and you can practice the preparation and delivery of a speech without feeling like you're on stage.

Being prepared for the small, uncomfortable next step in your journey is a big help in building your confidence with it. If your next step is a prepared 5-minute speech at Toast Masters, practice it in front of your family or a couple of friends. Each time you practice, the material becomes more familiar and your delivery improves. If you practice often enough, you'll come to know the material really well and be able to deliver it even without a script or prompt cards.

Look for ways to learn about the next difficult task that you can pursue before facing it directly. Are there books you can read that will give you pointers? Do some research online: there are innumerable websites offering free content for just about every task. For example, reading up on public speaking tips will help the unfamiliar to seem just a little bit more familiar and make the uncomfortable just a little less uncomfortable. I just did a Google search for "public speaking tips" and Google returned literally 760,000,000 results.

Now that you've broken the uncomfortable thing into smaller steps that you can approach individually and build up your capability incrementally, you can apply an experimental approach.

For the next step or two, define a hypothesis and desired learning outcome. Continuing with the public speaking example, your next step might be the prepared 5-minute speech. A hypothesis that might work could be:

GROWTH IS NOT COMFORTABLE

I believe that delivering a 5-minute prepared speech at Toast Masters will provide feedback that helps me to learn and improves my confidence with public speaking. I'll know this is true when I deliver the next speech with less nervousness.

Having a hypothesis helps you prepare for your speech and makes sure you seek feedback afterwards (though you always get feedback from your prepared speeches at Toast Masters). It also helps you know how you will measure success – in this case, it is the level of nervousness at the following speech, so you'll need to pay attention to how nervous you are when you deliver it to have something to measure against.

Although quantitative success measures are more scientific than qualitative ones, it isn't always possible to base your success measures on pure numbers for the hypotheses you create for your development goals. A subjective measure like nervousness is okay here, as long as you pay attention and remember to assess it.

So you've decided to get outside your comfort zone in the area of public speaking, and you've broken it down to smaller steps that can help you develop towards the goal. The first step is a 5-minute prepared speech at Toast Masters where you have a safe environment and a supportive audience. Now the next thing is to solidify your learning.

Learning happens anyway when we try something new. You can't stop your brain from storing experiences as memories, but you want to maximise that learning for your comfort zone breaking activity.

Schedule some time with yourself immediately after the event to reflect and capture your learning, assess your success measure and think through what you will improve for the next time.

Understand that trying something new can be awkward and it can feel like you have not been very successful at the activity. This is especially true if you have stayed within your comfort zone for a while and most of what you've taken on has been things you're already good at. Rest assured that the more you throw yourself outside your comfort zone, the easier it gets to deal with the fact that you aren't so good at those things. You're doing this to learn, not to be awesome. If always appearing to be awesome is important to you, then you might find getting outside your comfort zone to be especially challenging.

Now you're ready and the Toast Masters meeting has arrived.

You assess your level of nervousness prior to commencing your prepared speech, and you decide that your nervousness is 8 out of 10.

You deliver your speech. There are a few nervous pauses and a number of 'ums' and 'ahs', but once you get going it starts to feel a bit better and overall it goes okay.

You receive feedback from the group relating to your stance and body language, the topic and material delivered and the use of expression and movement. All of the feedback is given very supportively and you feel great that you were able to take on this challenge and do okay.

Afterwards, you sit down and take some notes, capturing your 8 out of 10 nervousness rating and the feedback you were given, as well as a few self-observations about how it felt and where you think you might make changes in the preparation or delivery next time.

It doesn't actually matter how well you did at your speech – what you learned from the experience is much more important. Try to avoid any judgement of the success of the activity, and instead focus on the learning.

In addition to building a capability at the comfort zone breaking activity, you're also developing your experimentation muscle. Each of these small experiments has a double-edged learning benefit: you're learning about the thing you're improving, but you're also learning about the experimental approach.

Activity

Find your discomfort zone.

Take a moment to reflect on the things you are skilfully avoiding.

What are you procrastinating about?

What have you been putting off?

What leaves you feeling a little bit nervous or anxious?

Writing those things down names them and they become a little less intimidating.

Deciding to do one small thing that gets you closer will make them even less daunting, especially if that thing itself is not so terrifying. In this section we looked at public speaking as an example. Attending Toast Masters is really easy as you're not committing to speaking in public (yet!), just turning up.

Something I've been skilfully avoiding	

One small thing I can do that gets me closer	

When will I do it by?	

CHAPTER 8

MAKING SENSE

One of the most important aspects of approaching the world with an agile mindset is how you go about making sense of the system in which you find yourself.

An agile individual has the ability to make sense of their environment, culture, processes and practices in ways beyond 'how we've always done it'.

We are always making sense of our surroundings, whether we are conscious of it or not. Without consciously choosing how you will make sense of something, you fall back to the known patterns and keep doing what you've always done. This often means moving through life without ever seeing beyond what you've always seen, and missing out on some of the richest opportunities to learn and grow.

> *IF YOU DEFINE THE PROBLEM CORRECTLY, YOU ALMOST HAVE THE SOLUTION.*
> Steve Jobs

Sense-making is both an ability and an activity, whereby various tools and models are employed to help the agile individual see things differently.

It is important to understand that we are not looking for the right way to see a situation when we are trying to make sense of it. The outcome when we apply a sense-making tool is to see the situation from another angle, allowing us to see aspects of it that were previously hidden.

Each tool is useful in a given context, but none of them will give an absolutely correct view. Most situations benefit from using more than one sense-making tool so you enable multiple views that each expose different elements.

Most of these tools are simple enough to get started with, but difficult to master, so even if you find there is not a lot of benefit when you use them the first few times, keep trying! The more you master their application and deepen your understanding of how they can be applied, the better your outcomes from using them will be, and the deeper the insights that will emerge.

How the brain makes sense of the world

Let's examine how the brain makes sense of its surroundings.

I'm not a neuroscientist, psychiatrist or a psychologist, and my understanding of the inner workings of the brain is certain to be flawed in many areas, but through years of study, reading and observation I have arrived at an understanding that is useful when dealing with others and reflecting on myself.

The brain is basically a pattern-matching system. Different reasoning pathways emerge depending on the type of pattern matched.

When input arrives through any of the 5 senses, the primitive parts of the brain receive it first and try to match it with known patterns. The input is then passed to other parts of the brain depending on what is perceived.

The brain prioritises survival above everything else, so when an input matching a memory of something dangerous is perceived – whether it's a predatorial beast or a nasty interaction with another person in the office – the brain takes emergency action telling the adrenal glands to dump cortisol and adrenalin into the system in readiness for a life-threatening situation. Together these hormones prepare the body to take action by increasing blood sugar and blood flow to the muscles, and reducing the action of systems that are less essential for survival like digestion, the immune system and thinking.

The brain doesn't know the difference between a life-threatening predator and a connection-threatening social interaction. Both threats bring about similar responses and the same dump of hormones. What this means for us in today's world, where we are not so likely to face predatorial beasts, is the need to recognise that consistently high

IF YOU CHANGE THE WAY YOU LOOK AT THINGS, THE THINGS YOU LOOK AT CHANGE.
Wayne Dyer

stress over the long term can be immensely damaging to a person's wellbeing. High levels of cortisol are associated with weight gain, high blood pressure, osteoporosis, thinning of the skin and susceptibility for bruising, muscle weakness, mood swings, anxiety, depression, irritability, reduced cognitive function and reduced immune system function.

The brain's second priority is the conservation of energy. When you're resting, the brain uses around one-fifth of your total energy consumption just maintaining and balancing its own electrical system. So the prioritisation of rest makes sense, but it also leads to a natural tendency to cut corners.

The next priority is to create standard operating procedures, so that neurons that regularly fire together have their connections strengthened in ways that allow them to fire together faster and with less energy expenditure.

Creating habits is the next priority for the brain. Any activity that is repeated often enough is laid down as a habit. This is very good for efficiency and for conserving energy. If you had to think through tying your shoelaces every time as if it were the first time, you would have to expend a lot more thought and energy.

Another of the brain's priorities is to use the whole brain. When complex tasks are being undertaken, the brain spreads the load – and under EEG we can see activity across areas of the brain not directly implicated in the execution of that task.

One thing to note through all these priorities is that while the brain is amazingly capable at multi-tasking when it comes to regulatory activities, it cannot multi-task at all when it comes to higher cognitive functions. The brain can only do one thing at a time when it involves thinking. Many people will tell you they are good at multi-tasking, but they are really just slicing those tasks into small activities and executing them one at a time. This leads to context switching and increases the time it would take to complete those same tasks individually while also reducing the quality.

Once you understand the brain's need to conserve energy, take shortcuts and build habits, you can appreciate the brain's preference to always do the least-energetic thing it can get away with. This means that the brain will always offer a quick response to any stimulus. This is great when you're tying your shoes, but not so great when you need to be creative or innovative.

> EIGHTY-FIVE PERCENT OF THE REASONS FOR FAILURE ARE DEFICIENCIES IN THE SYSTEMS AND PROCESS RATHER THAN THE EMPLOYEE. THE ROLE OF MANAGEMENT IS TO CHANGE THE PROCESS RATHER THAN BADGERING INDIVIDUALS TO DO BETTER.
> W. Edwards Deming

It takes effort to put your brain into thinking gear and not simply look for a mental short-cut. You need to be mindful of what is happening inside your own head to know that the task at hand deserves a little more effort, energy and thought.

Activity

Reflect for a moment on a recent time when you were placed under stress, especially if it was the kind of stress that could be seen as a threat, such as a threat to your livelihood by displeasing your boss or a threat to social connection from a heated argument with your partner.

How did you feel? What happened to your thinking? What was the end result?

Make some notes.

Stressor	Feeling	Thinking	Result

Your feelings and thoughts were probably your brain taking the shortest and most efficient path to a reaction that would keep you safe. The way you responded to those feelings and thoughts determined the result you got.

If you continue to react the way you've always reacted, you'll continue to get the results you've always gotten.

MAKING SENSE

Making sense of those feelings and thoughts helps you to reflect on what you might have done differently if you chose another way to look at the stressor.

For each of the stressors you described above, identify another perspective you could have taken that would allow you to see it differently. If you did look at it differently, what change would that bring to your feelings and thoughts? What would it mean for the end result?

Stressor	New perspective	Feeling	Thinking	Result

CHAPTER 9
COGNITIVE BIASES

An agile individual is aware of their biases.

A bias is a leaning towards a particular direction. We could say that a car with a deflated front left tyre has a bias towards the left, because if we don't hold the steering wheel tightly it would go to the left.

A cognitive bias is the same thing applied to our thinking. It is a set of mental patterns that pull our thinking in a particular direction. The difficulty with a cognitive bias is that it isn't as easy to see. We can see when a car pulls to the left when we are driving it, even if we can't see the deflated tyre. When we are in the car, we readily observe the tendency to veer to the left.

> A GREAT MANY PEOPLE THINK THEY ARE THINKING WHEN THEY ARE MERELY REARRANGING THEIR PREJUDICES.
> William James

In our own thinking, it is much more difficult to see our own habits and tendencies. Unlike the car, we are not aware that we are thinking to the left – and while we can get outside the car to check on the tyre, we cannot easily get outside ourselves. It takes a very conscious effort at self-reflection and repeated intentional activity to be able to see our own biases.

Even after years of self-reflection and deliberate practice at developing a mindset that is not hampered by bias, we will continue to fall into our biases from time to time, especially when we are triggered by events or difficulties.

Being agile requires us to be aware of what bias is and – through that awareness and self-reflection – to be aware of when we are leaning in a particular direction due to our biases.

Confirmation bias

The most readily-identifiable bias is confirmation bias. This is the mental pattern that seeks to match what we observe to what we already know. It is basically the brain taking mental shortcuts and is a strong survival instinct. If we had to assess everything we observe before being able to know how to respond, we'd get eaten by the first predators that come along. The brain needs a way to respond immediately to inputs that match patterns representing danger.

Matching an input to a known danger happens in the primitive parts of the brain. The amygdala and hippocampus conspire to set in place a reaction to an input long before it ever gets to the frontal cortex. The primitive parts of the brain have memory and emotion, but they lack logic or language. They have much more influence in our decisions than the frontal cortex where logic resides, simply because they receive all sensory inputs first.

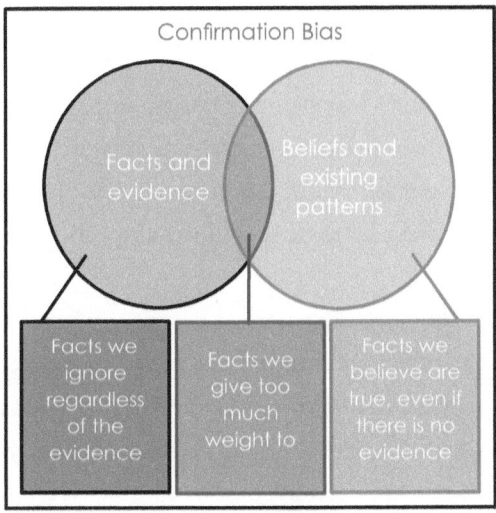

That ability of the brain to respond immediately to danger in the primitive landscape translates to the way we make decisions in the modern world, even though we are not facing the same dangers.

With confirmation bias, we typically accept whatever matches our existing patterns as the truth (even if it is not true), and discount what does not match those patterns (even if it is true.)

It is important to understand confirmation bias in ourselves and in others, especially when we are discussing something about which multiple parties feel strongly and see differently. Facts will not sway an argument when people are working from a confirmation bias, and most people are in a confirmation bias most of the time.

If you are discussing something with someone and it appears that you both have differing views, remember confirmation bias. Is it possible that your view being different to the other person's view and their comments seeming to go against what you know to be true is triggering a confirmation bias for you? Are you discounting the points they are raising because they don't align to your existing ideas?

Maybe the other person is stuck in a pattern of confirmation bias, or maybe you yourself are. How do you tell? Get as objective as you can with the details. Is it even remotely possible that their points are true? Even if they fly in the face of what you know, take a moment to examine their argument as if it were true.

If you can be sure that your argument is based on solid objective facts, you still can't be sure that you're not stuck in a confirmation bias, especially if it is something you feel strongly about. Remember that even objective facts may turn out to be proven wrong in the future. If you were arguing that the world is a sphere with someone who believes it to be flat, no facts will sway how they feel. Any points you make about the ability to fly a plane in one direction and end up where you started, or the visible curvature of the earth through the plane's window may be vehemently discounted as the lies of a conspiracy theory. How might a person who hasn't travelled in a plane know that they could be wrong, and you might be right?

That last point is worth repeating. How do *you* know that they are wrong, and you are right?

Maybe you do know and maybe you are right, but that isn't helpful. Being right isn't going to help you or the other person if you each believe something different.

There are two very useful tools you can use when caught up in a discussion where you both have opposing views and you both feel that your opinion is based on fact:

1. Elevate the argument.
2. Take the other person's point of view.

We'll look into these later in this chapter.

Egocentric bias

Egocentric bias is a mental pattern where we place a higher value on our own perspective than on facts or evidence.

We see egocentric bias quite readily in others: these are the people who seem to have a deep-seated need to be right and feel they are always right, regardless of how obvious the facts are.

Egocentric bias, by its very nature, is much more difficult to observe in ourselves. When we feel we are right, the mental patterns that support our feelings are the very same ones that prevent us from seeing that we are stuck in an egocentric bias.

Egocentric bias can be initiated when we take an exaggerated impression of our own contribution to an outcome compared to the contributions of others. This is not always unhealthy or entirely due to an over-inflated ego. It can result from a situation where we have strenuously pushed ourselves to achieve an outcome that didn't appear to have the same level of effort from others or where we didn't have visibility of how vigorously others worked. We know how hard we worked, and we sometimes feel that our contribution was the key element that resulted in success. Without us, the result would not have been achieved.

The egocentric part comes in when we don't take into account the possibility that others were striving just as hard as we were, perhaps even assuming that the efforts they contributed that we didn't have visibility of didn't occur.

As with confirmation bias, the key to helping avoid egocentric bias in yourself is self-observation and self-reflection.

Any time you feel you are absolutely right about something, you may be in an egocentric bias pattern, taking your own thoughts as correct and discounting the perspective of others.

Group think

Group think is a cognitive bias where we adapt our thinking to suit the group.

Often called 'anchoring,' it appears within a group discussion. A more senior or experienced member of the group might express a view about the topic, leading others in the group to anchor their thinking on that view.

We all have a deep-seated need to fit in. This is another survival instinct that has kept us safe through our evolution because a tribe of humans is much more likely to support individual survival than if we were to live alone. That need to fit in prevents us from saying or doing anything that might endanger our acceptance by the group. When we are new to a group and still trying to identify how we fit in, we are especially susceptible to group think. It can be very difficult to speak out with an idea that goes against what the group thinks when we are new to the group.

In society, group think rears its head in ways that can constrain the opportunities of the group to learn or collaborate with others. Many groups create stereotypes aimed at anyone who is not part of the group, labelling them as being stupid, lazy, immoral, or simply wrong. Religious groups, political parties and street gangs share the idea that they have the moral high ground and everyone else is sinful, wrong or at least mistaken.

When psychological safety is low, group think is high. When the environment is psychologically safe, you can say whatever you think; even if it's only half-thought through or a bit daft, it is perfectly acceptable for your thinking to diverge from the group. When the environment isn't psychologically safe, it can damage your standing with the group to say anything that might turn out to be wrong, is not fully thought through or goes against what the senior people in the group think.

Group think increases as motivation reduces: when people in the group don't care about the topic of a conversation, they'll just go with whatever the group thinks, even if they know it is a daft idea or they can think of something better.

Groups that value seeking harmony over innovation or creativity are especially susceptible to group think. When the priority is for everyone to get along nicely, everyone is hyper-aware of not saying anything that might ruffle feathers or goes against what the rest of the group are saying. Harmony is important, but elevating the value of harmony over the value of finding better answers leads to a set of behaviours based on conformity. We lose a lot of diversity of thought when the groups prioritises conformity ahead of diversity.

When consensus is the approach to decision making, we see an increase in group think. Knowing that the only way we'll get to a decision is if everyone agrees ensures people who have mildly divergent ideas will remain silent. They would rather accept the idea being proposed than have the conversation go on indefinitely, so they keep their ideas to themselves.

Groups that have been through a period of conflict can slip into a stance of conflict avoidance, increasing the propensity of group think. Such a group has felt the discomfort of overblown conflict and will now do anything to avoid it returning. If accepting the idea under discussion will prevent a conflict, they will accept it, even if they know there is a better idea.

Group think increases when we don't have equal voice. If there are people in the group who command most of the speaking time – either because they are the more senior in the group and have the most experience in the subject matter or because they are more passionate – then there will be people in the group who do not have much speaking time. When we don't have equal voice, the quiet people may not feel comfortable speaking out their ideas. Maybe it is simply due to the quieter people being more introverted, or maybe they are new to the group and unsure of where they stand. In either case, this leads to them not voicing their ideas and can put the group into group think.

There are any number of facilitation techniques that can help to reduce or eliminate group think when you are the facilitator, but the key thing for an agile individual is to be aware of group think and to be able to identify when it is occurring in themselves or others.

Identifying when you are in the grip of group think is not easy. The feeling that goes along with being in the group and the need to belong can leave you feeling that the group is right. Those feelings can be well supported by facts, even if those facts are entirely subjective or simply rationalisations.

There are a number of questions you can consider to assess whether you are being truly open to divergent thinking and accepting of all ideas or whether you are stuck in a group think cycle.

- Do we have equal voice?
- Do we have psychological safety?
- Are we creating assumptions or stereotypes about those outside our group?
- Are we over-indexing on creating harmony?
- Are we avoiding conflict?
- Are we trying to achieve consensus?
- Is everyone fully bought into the conversation?
- Are some of us moderating our input in order to fit in with the group?

Do we have equal voice?

Checking for equal voice is something you want to do in every group, even if you are not the facilitator. Some people are naturally more introverted than others and, in any group, people will fill a range of positions between introverted and extroverted.

Simply counting the number of words each participant in the group offers to the conversation can give you a surprising picture of how equal each person's voice is. It isn't an absolute – some people use fewer words than others to express themselves but still have equal involvement and may even have a more significant impact on the conversation. While you can't make decisions blindly based on the result, it is an interesting picture of how balanced the conversation is and invites you to assess how equally the conversation is going.

COGNITIVE BIASES

Even without any empirical evidence, you can still observe the group to see if everyone is equally engaged and ready to offer their thinking. Are there people in the group who are remaining mostly silent? Is there anyone who hasn't spoken for a while?

Do we have psychological safety?

Consider the question of psychological safety. It is a very tricky area to observe and understand the true level of psychological safety. You can't simply ask others, "How safe do we feel to say what we really think?" When the environment is not safe, people will generally say that it is safe because they feel unsafe to say that it isn't.

There are times when you would expect psychological safety to be low and accept that it cannot be instantly improved. When a team is newly-formed or a group has been brought together that don't know each other, psychological safety will be low. People still need to get to know each other and will have their polite mask on. There are ways to improve psychological safety, but they take time. If this is a newly-formed group, give it time and be aware that you cannot expect too much in the way of psychological safety.

When Google published the results of their Project Aristotle, they cited psychological safety as the most important attribute of high-performing teams and a foundational attribute for other attributes that support high performance such as dependability, clarity, meaning and impact.

So, if psychological safety is so important, but you can't just ask if people feel safe, how do you go about assessing it? Here are a few things to look out for in any group discussion that will help you to understand the level of safety.

Some people are not speaking much and don't ask questions. This is a reasonably obvious sign and can be observed when you have a senior person in the group leading the conversation. Is anyone questioning their assertions? If the content of their contribution to the conversation is completely positive, obvious and aligns with what everyone is thinking, then it might be reasonable to expect that there would not be any reason to challenge what they are saying, but ask yourself: is everyone truly going along with everything being said? If not, and there are not many questions, it might not be a safe environment.

When there are no disagreements, then it might be a sign of a lack of psychological safety. It could also be a sign that the meeting should have been an email, but if you are in a session that deserves to be a meeting, you are probably trying to work something out or come to some decision as a group. When psychological safety is high, there will be disagreements on particular points and some back and forth in the discussion. When psychological safety is low, you'll notice there are very few disagreements.

People stay 'in their box.' This symptom of low psychological safety shows up when people are reluctant to venture outside their role, limiting their contribution to the areas that they are involved with and not exploring the contributions of others. Even if people are in strongly-defined roles, it is still important to understand what others are doing and how it fits in with their own activities. If nobody is asking about what others are working on, it could be a sign of low psychological safety.

Groups that have high levels of psychological safety find it easy to own up to mistakes. When safety is high, and a mistake is discovered, it is easy to take ownership of the mistake because there will not be any humiliation or shame – just an acknowledgement that we need to fix it and a decision as to what we will do about it. It doesn't even feel like owning up; it is just sharing something that the group needs to know in order to resolve a difficulty.

When psychological safety is low, feedback is not valued. Feedback is the loving gift that helps us to improve, but in many environments, it is not given or received well. If feedback is used as a weapon to put people down or received as a sign of criticism or inadequacy, then it will be avoided.

If you find people are not asking each other for help, it could be a sign of low psychological safety. Asking for help requires a certain amount of vulnerability, and it can feel like you're admitting that you are not capable of doing something on your own. The opposite is true: it takes self-knowledge and courage to know that you would benefit from help and additionally, it shares opportunities to learn. Both parties will learn from the work when helping each other. Groups with high psychological safety will often ask each other for help.

When discussions are dominated by the more senior members of the group, with little in the way of contribution or questions from the less senior members of the group, you may have a low level of psychological safety. Groups with high levels of psychological safety value the discussion and welcome questions or comments from their less experienced members. It helps the less experienced person to learn but it also helps the group to see the situation in a new light from the questions that arise from the person with the fresh perspective.

Are we creating assumptions or stereotypes about those outside our group?

A possible sign of group think is when we cast assumptions or hold to stereotypes about those outside of the group.

This is easier to spot from outside the group as beliefs about others may have become a firmly held truth to those within the group. You can observe it from within the group if you are conscious of the language the group uses. Look for any language that discriminates, diminishes or dehumanises those outside the group – anything that indicates an 'us and them' mentality.

> MAN ACTS AS THOUGH HE WERE THE SHAPER AND MASTER OF LANGUAGE, WHILE IN FACT LANGUAGE REMAINS THE MASTER OF MAN
> Martin Heidegger

Some of the language that separates those within the group from those who are not in the group is easy to spot, but some is not obvious at all. Here are a few examples and some suggestions as to what you can replace them with in order to become less locked in stereotypes and assumptions about others.

Separation word	What it means	Suggested word
Customers	'Customers' is a term used to describe the people we serve, but they are not part of our group.	Use a term that brings them closer to your group. Use personas to give them a name and a personality so we can relate to them as people rather than think of them as outsiders.
Dependencies	Dependencies is fine when describing functions or features, but not when describing people. This is another example of 'us and them' language.	If the dependency is a Team, use the name of their Team, or if it is a person, use their name. If you don't know their name, that might be a sign that you don't know them as well as you should.
Drive	'Driving an outcome' is push language. If it were a bus and you were the driver, then everyone else is just a passenger.	Co-create instead!

Separation word	What it means	Suggested word
Get people on board	Getting people 'on board' means coercing them to buy into something that they were not a part of deciding.	Better to involve people in the decision – then you don't need to 'get them on board'
Motivate	'Motivating' is another word for getting people to do what you have decided they should do. People who are engaged with an outcome and invested in getting there don't need you to motivate them.	Clarity. Providing clarity on the outcomes that matter and why removes the need to motivate them.
Persuade	See "Get people on board"	Inspire

Separation word	What it means	Suggested word
Resources	'Resources' is often used in project management to separate those doing the work from those leading the project. Calling people resources trivialises their humanity and compares them to something we can dig out of the ground. Resources are fungible, they can be traded and if I trade one lump of coal for another lump of coal, I still have a lump of coal and there has been very little impact. People are not fungible; I cannot trade one person out of a Team for another person with a similar skill set without negatively impacting the Team.	People
Sell	See "Get people on board"	Listen

Separation word	What it means	Suggested word
Stakeholders	Stakeholders is, "Us and them," language, indicating that they are somehow external to the in-group who are doing the work.	Use descriptive terms that bring them closer such as, 'the broader project team,' 'people impacted by ...,' or 'people interested in our success.'
Tell	See "Get people on board"	Invite
They, their, them	They, their and them are separation words, whoever 'they' are they are not one of us.	Use their name.
Users	'Users' describes the people who will use the thing we are delivering, but it creates separation between us and them, they are just users as if they are on drugs.	Design a persona and give them a name, i.e. Hari, then you can call them Hari instead of user.
We, us, our, (when used for our group)	You might be surprised to see 'we' in this list. 'We' separates us into people who are "one of us" and everyone else.	Be descriptive of our group, if we are the Team then use that, save 'we' for times when you're describing everyone.

COGNITIVE BIASES

Are we too focused on creating harmony or avoiding conflict?

Some groups get so caught up with creating harmony that they cannot challenge each other or disagree about anything. This can bring about strong instances of group think.

Disagreement need not lead to disharmony. It is very healthy to have constructive challenge of ideas in a group.

Of course, we do want to build harmony within the group, but we don't want to do that at the expense of open and creative conversation. You can have harmony in a group that doesn't feel the same way about every topic.

A lack of constructive challenge in a conversation may be a sign that the group has over-invested in harmony and fallen into a pattern of group think.

If you witness this in a group you are working with or a part of, throw out a challenge: ask the focus of the conversation in the opposite way to how the conversation has it framed.

Are we seeking consensus?

Seeking consensus may be effective in some groups, but it might also lead to group think.

When we need to achieve consensus in order to move on from a topic, we can end up in endless discussions that go nowhere. Eventually, some of the voices will be shut off purely from fatigue and a desire to just make a decision. When psychological safety and equal voice are high, attempting to achieve consensus can still lock you into a pattern of group think.

If you observe this happening in your group, see if participants can agree to consent over consensus. When we have consent over consensus, we agree that no decision will be taken that goes directly against something anyone in the group feels strongly about – but if it is something you can still consent to, we'll take the decision and move forward.

Is everyone fully invested?

If there are people involved in the conversation who are not invested in it, they may have less interest in the outcome and will go along with whatever the group comes up with.

You'll be able to observe this when there are people who offer little in the way of input or seem to sit quietly without building on the conversation.

Body language can also be a giveaway: people tend to sit back when they are not invested in the conversation, they are less animated and less likely to be giving their attention to whoever is speaking.

In some meetings where people have their computers with them, or in online meetings, some participants could be multi-tasking, listening with only a small portion of their attention as they do their email or work on some other task. Use your intuition: if you notice somebody's body language and it feels like they are not invested, you are probably right.

If you feel that there is someone who is not invested, it might not be wise to call them out on their level of interest, but it can be effective to directly seek their opinion. Simply asking, "What do you think Jane?" could be all it takes to bring them back into the conversation.

Are some of us trying to fit in?

Sometimes group think emerges because one or more of us is trying to fit into the group.

When there are people who have only recently joined the group, their natural tendency is to avoid ruffling any feathers as they try to figure out how they fit in.

Even when people have been with the group for a reasonable time, some people will always moderate their behaviour and language to fit in with the group. This is just who they are and their natural approach to being in groups. It is not a negative thing at all. Humans are social creatures with a need to be accepted by the group.

Are we avoiding conflict?

Topics being 'off the table' for discussion is another sign of low psychological safety. You need to know the group reasonably well to know if there are topics they are avoiding because of past conflicts or maybe they feel powerless to impact a topic and the frustration they feel about it relegates it to the conversation they can't have. This can become the elephant in the room, a difficulty the group has been facing for some time that continues to go unsaid. When there are topics the group cannot bring themselves to discuss, you may find you have a low level of psychological safety.

Dealing with biases

An agile individual is aware of bias and the impact it has in keeping us from growing and trying new ways of doing things, they can deal with bias in themselves and in others.

When you find yourself faced with biases, whether in yourself or in others, there are some tried and tested techniques to help reduce the impact of bias, even if you can't eliminate it all together.

The difficulty in dealing with biases is not the action to take as much as the identification of the bias in the first place. It can be easy to label a behaviour in another person as a bias when it doesn't align with your needs or expectations, but the other person may have a deeper understanding of the situation at hand and your expectation may be the result of your own bias.

COGNITIVE BIASES

Be mindful of the possibility of your own biases. Even when it feels like you are absolutely clear of bias and completely supported by the facts of a situation, there remains a possibility that you are operating with bias. Keeping that in mind will help you to respond with the appropriate level of action.

Elevate the argument

Elevating the argument means lifting the viewpoint of the discussion until you reach a point where you can both agree.

Imagine you are discussing whether agile approaches will help a team to deliver high quality. You are pointing out the practices, processes and empirical results achieved by other teams. The other person is expressing their dissatisfaction with the lack of rigour, insufficient planning, poor documentation and gung-ho attitude of a team they worked with.

Your argument is based on fact: you've worked with teams that delivered extremely high quality using agile approaches, with good rigour, sufficient planning, great documentation and very high quality.

Their argument is also based on fact: they have experienced for themselves the difficulties faced by the team they worked with.

Elevating the argument means stepping out of the points scoring and the detail until you find a basis for common ground.

You might say, "Can we at least agree that we are both interested in helping teams deliver high quality products?"

If you can agree on something that is an elevated aspect of both of your viewpoints, no matter how small it might be, then you radically change the nature of the conversation. Instead of facing each other with pressure and resistance, now you can both face into the discussion together. You have created an alliance to explore the details together to see what will emerge.

Now that you are both facing into the discussion together, you can explore each of the points in a different way. "You mentioned documentation… What happened for the team you worked with?"

Take the other person's point of view

Whenever you are discussing something with someone and you both have opposing points of view, you might feel the other person is not taking your view into account, but are you taking their view seriously?

Remember, being right is not especially valuable if you don't have alignment. You might need to step back from the need to be right so that you can first seek some common ground.

Seeking common ground can be difficult when you are both passionate about the topic and confident in your position. If the other person is passionate about their viewpoint, don't expect them to step back from it, the simplest thing is for you to step back from your view.

COGNITIVE BIASES

First, join the other person in their viewpoint. Instead of trying to score points that prove your point of view, you ask exploratory questions that help you to understand the other person's position.

To effectively explore the other person's perspective, you need to be aware of your own patterns and behaviours. If you're entering the conversation with a need to prove your point, then it can be very difficult to free yourself from your proving patterns, but it is worth it.

Clearing yourself of the need to prove you are right opens the door to improve your understanding. Even if it turns out that you are right, your understanding of how you know you are right will be improved by exploring the other person's thoughts and feelings with full acceptance that they have a valid reason to feel the way they do.

When you're exploring the other person's point of view, be careful with the type of questions you ask. Asking 'why' someone feels a particular way about the topic can easily be taken as a confrontational challenge of their view with an implication that they are somehow inferior for feeling the way they do. This will not allow you to establish a rapport or get into the conversation deeply enough for the other person to fully open up their thinking to you.

Sometimes you want to know why they feel the way they do so you can understand the information they base their belief upon. If you need to know why, convert it into a 'what' question. Instead of asking, "Why do you think…" try, "What is it about…"

One of the simplest ways to open up the conversation, is to ask, "… Tell me more." Use your own words, but the intent is to demonstrate that you have heard the other person and would like to understand more deeply without challenging them or implying that they are wrong. This is especially important early in the conversation as the supporting information they share might actually indicate that they are not wrong, or at least help you to understand how they can feel the way they do when it contradicts all the evidence as you see it.

"You mentioned that …, tell me more."

"I'm interested in the point you raised about …, tell me more."

"I have never experienced …, tell me more."

"I've heard of that before, but I don't know much about it. Tell me more."

When you have listened with compassion and demonstrated an interest in what the other person thinks and feels, without any need to prove they are wrong or you are right, you will develop an understanding of what they think and an empathy for how they feel. You are viewing the topic from their angle.

Once you can see the situation from their point of view, you can start to establish some common ground. Whatever the differences between your two viewpoints, there will be some similarities as well, even if you must get creative in your descriptions in order to find them.

When viewed from the perspective of common ground, both viewpoints become easier to understand to the other person and the conversation changes.

By consciously stepping back from your own confirmation bias, you have enabled a new angle in the conversation that allowed you both to come together for a mutual understanding of the commonalities between your arguments so you can look at both perspectives. This allows the other person to view the topic from a position that isn't so firmly entrenched behind their own confirmation bias. You've helped them to see the situation differently, by firstly seeing the situation differently yourself.

This rapport will allow you to invite them to see it from your angle. That needn't be a direct invitation to see it from your point of view, even with some rapport built, a direct invitation can create a barrier between you. It can be established as a series of steps building on their position with small incremental steps towards your position.

Valuing divergent thinking

Divergent thinking happens when our thinking goes down different paths. It doesn't mean we are disagreeing necessarily, just thinking differently.

Thinking differently allows us to capture our ideas without anchoring our thoughts to the ideas of others. Additionally, when we bring that divergent thinking together as a group, the thoughts people share will trigger new thinking in others.

The easiest way to encourage divergent thinking is simply to celebrate it when it occurs. When someone in the group offers an idea that helps the group to think differently about the topic, thank them for their contribution by explicitly calling out the fact that it has helped us to take a new idea into our thinking.

> A DISCERNING MIND PURSUING DIVERGENT THINKING IS THE CRUCIBLE THAT STEWS CREATIVITY AND MEANING IN LIFE.
> Abhinav Saxena

When facilitating any sort of meeting where we are creating something or working through a solution to an issue, there are times when it can be valuable for the group to diverge so we capture everyone's contributions without the influence of group think before then converging again to bring all that divergent thinking together again. Post-It® notes are brilliant for this: they allow each person to capture their own thinking and when we converge, you can organise the contributions into clusters of similar ideas, vote on them, rank them or put them into a model.

Valuing divergent thinking also means valuing diversity in the group. Sometimes everyone in a group is so similar that there really isn't any diversity of thought.

Often the people we invite into the group are very similar to the people already in the group. We see this when hiring managers try to find people who are a cultural match for the group so that it is easier for them to fit in and less disruptive when they join. This creates a significant limitation in the potential for diversity of thought and opportunities for creativity in the group.

Valuing fresh perspectives

Fresh perspectives bring a particular type of divergent thinking to the group.

Valuing fresh perspectives means bringing in ways for the group to see the situation from a different viewpoint, reframing the situation or bringing in completely new ideas.

New people bring new ideas and new ways of looking at things. They may not have all of the context of a situation, but their thinking hasn't been

> THE DIFFICULTY LIES NOT SO MUCH IN DEVELOPING NEW IDEAS AS IN ESCAPING FROM OLD ONES.
> John Maynard Keynes

clouded by the same issues either. They bring a fresh set of experiences and another way of thinking to the group.

Valuing fresh perspectives doesn't mean that you should regularly get rid of more experienced people and replace them with fresh people. That would be immensely disruptive and break down cohesion in the group. What it means is to listen to those in the group who may have less experience. Their fresh perspective may shine a light on the situation that allows you to see it from another angle.

When you're faced with a situation in which all group members have a lot of experience, you might want to bring in an external voice. Invite someone from another team into your group discussion. In complex environments where teams depend on other teams, it can be immensely valuable to bring in the perspective of someone in one of those other teams.

Valuing psychological safety

If you value psychological safety, you'll want to ensure that everyone feels completely safe to say what they really think, even if it is not fully thought through or even if it is wrong.

When you value psychological safety, you don't view any input whatsoever as being wrong – it is just a thought that was shared.

If you suspect that psychological safety is low, you can collect inputs to a discussion or votes on a decision in secret. There are many systems that allow this. One of the simplest is email.

Ask participants in a discussion to send their inputs to the discussion to you by email in advance, encouraging them not to 'reply all.' It can be a good idea to let people know that you're doing this in order to increase safety and that their points will be raised at the meeting, but not the identity of who raised the point. This will not only raise the safety level and allow inputs that people might not be comfortable to raise when they are in the conversation, it also avoids anchoring and group think.

COGNITIVE BIASES

If there is a decision to be made that you have some clear choices for but either a low or uncertain level of psychological safety, a proven technique is a secret ballot.

There are many online tools that can enable this for a virtual vote or you can simply have people write down their choices on a Post-It® note or piece of paper and collect and tally the votes without exposing how each individual voted. You can simplify the process by giving each option being voted on a number.

When psychological safety is low and you're seeing the symptoms mentioned above, encourage some disagreement. This involves offering a comment that most participants in the discussion will not agree with – don't make it combative or inflammatory, just a little bit wrong. If you're discussing how to resolve something that went pear-shaped for example, suggest we do nothing.

You'll need to be on your toes facilitating this to ensure it doesn't descend into anything destructive, but it can be a very effective technique to get people talking, add some energy into the discussion and create opportunities to call out safety and celebrate it.

Valuing equal voice

Ensuring equal voice is another area for reducing group think and other biases.

Equal voice ensures you hear from everyone in the group, bringing all perspectives into the discussion. Sometimes the quiet people are not confident in their ideas but they have the kernel of a thought that will trigger the next best idea in the group.

If you're counting the contributions of participants, either in the number of times they speak or the number of words they offer the conversation, and you notice there are one or two people who are contributing much less often, simply asking for their thoughts could bring them into the discussion so their ideas can be heard.

> ALLOW ALL THE GOVERNED AN EQUAL VOICE IN THE GOVERNMENT, AND THAT, AND THAT ONLY, IS SELF-GOVERNMENT.
> Abraham Lincoln

Observe carefully before calling on an individual by name. There may be a reason they are being quieter. Possibly they don't feel safe or they are new to the group and unsure how to contribute. Maybe they are not especially engaged or the conversation doesn't involve their area of knowledge. They might be unsure of the context or they could be being drowned out by the louder more enthusiastic participants.

Whatever the reason for them being quieter, you still want to hear their views. Even if the topic is outside their expertise they will at least offer another perspective.

Calling on them to provide their viewpoint needs to be done sensitively and doesn't put them on the spot if they have nothing to offer

COGNITIVE BIASES

or have no knowledge at all of the background. You don't want to be the one that asks them for their view and they sit there uncomfortably with nothing to offer except their own embarrassment.

Activity

This week, do something that will help you to deal with biases.

Choose something from each of the areas below and define something concrete that you will do to improve it.

Technique for dealing with biases	What I will do to apply this technique
Elevate the argument	
Take the other person's point of view	
Value divergent thinking	
Value fresh perspectives	

Value psychological safety	
Value equal voice	

CHAPTER 10

FEEDBACK

Feedback is your friend.

Knowing that change is inevitable, expecting it and even creating it so you can harness the positive benefits is all well and good, but what do you do to create change? What change should you be working towards creating?

Without clarity of what needs to change, you could be creating change that is not contributing to your goals – or worse still, it might even be creating damage.

There is a lot throughout this book and any number of others about the importance of having a purpose and a vision so you can plan for changes that will align to your purpose and contribute towards your vision, but all of those things can be tainted by your own perspective and clouded by cognitive biases.

Whatever your purpose and your vision, the most valuable places to bring about change for good is change within yourself. Learning and growth should always be high priorities for the agile individual.

Choosing what to learn is still difficult and fraught with opportunities to go in a direction that is not conducive to where you want to go, especially when where you want to go is in a direction where you will trip over your own blind spots about who you really are as a person and how you fit into your own reality.

This is where feedback comes in.

Feedback is the mechanism through which you can learn and improve in ways you will not be able to envision yourself.

Feedback is a loving gift

Feedback is the loving gift that provides something you might otherwise be blind to.

We all have our blind spots, things about ourselves and the way we operate that we simply cannot see on our own and there is no mirror we can hold up to ourselves that will expose those blind spots.

Feedback is the mirror through which we can see ourselves in ways beyond our normal self-image, providing ample opportunities for us to grow and improve how we operate.

FEEDBACK

Not all feedback is useful, however. Sometimes the person providing the feedback is looking through their own blind spots or expressing some bias of their own construction. The tricky thing is knowing when feedback is useful and when it is just the outpouring of someone else's state of mind.

In order to determine if feedback is useful and something you can utilise for self-improvement, you must first reflect on the feedback. Is it even slightly possible that it is accurate? Even if it is not accurate, could it be valuable? What would you do differently if it is?

It is very tempting when we first hear feedback to dismiss it, thinking that the person providing the feedback is stupid or simply wrong. Your first response should be to consider the feedback as a loving gift. This can help you move past that initial response and look for the goodness within the words.

Asking for feedback can be incredibly uncomfortable for some people and it can even bring about feelings of anxiety. This is not unusual, but it is something to work through as avoiding feedback could be robbing you of opportunities to grow.

If you're feeling weak at the knees at the thought of asking someone for feedback, don't let that hold you back. It gets easier every time you do it.

The way you ask for feedback is important; it establishes the thinking process that the person giving you the feedback will utilise when formulating their response.

There are two main ways you can go about asking for feedback: structured feedback or the spontaneous discussion.

The spontaneous discussion is 'in the moment' relative to a specific event or activity. After completing something you're working on with a colleague, you might ask them how they felt you went with a particular task.

This approach can be very valuable, especially if you don't wait for the end of a big project, but ask for feedback regularly at the conclusion of small tasks. That way you'll have the opportunity to course correct while you're still working on the project.

It would be a tragedy to learn about something that could have been improved but now it's too late and not relevant to your next project.

If you're learning a new skill or recently moved into a new role, opportunities to ask for unstructured spontaneous feedback will be many. Ask how you performed with each small incremental improvement or each new thing you've learned as you practice it. Asking "How do you think I went with …?" or "What could I have done differently or better that would have improved the outcome when I was …?"

Often when learning a new skill, you won't have to ask for feedback at all – hopefully you have a leader or mentor you are working with that will freely offer you feedback as you go. If you're

FEEDBACK

lucky enough to be in this situation, value it and be grateful for the care and attention the other person is giving you as they share their learning with you and help you to get better at the new skill or role.

The trick can be to be present enough in the moment to recognise what you are being told as feedback. Sometimes it feels like criticism, nagging, or disapproval. You might feel that whatever you do, the other person is never satisfied and nothing you ever do is good enough. Feeling this way about the feedback you receive will see you shrinking back from it. Try your best to view it as constructive feedback, even if the other person is not very good at giving feedback and their tone of voice makes it sound judgemental. This allows you to receive it as the loving gift it should be and to use it for helping you to know what needs to improve in your performance.

Structured feedback takes a little more preparation, but it is worth it. When seeking structured feedback, follow these few pointers to help you make the most of the learning that will come your way.

- Schedule a time to ask for feedback
- Think through what you want to ask
- Listen
- Take notes
- Clarify the feedback so you're sure what they're saying
- Be grateful

Schedule a time to ask for feedback

Unlike spontaneous feedback, structured feedback is a deeper conversation that you don't want to miss out on because the right moment doesn't arrive.

Schedule a time to ask another person for feedback. Choose a time that works for both of you, being sensitive to the demands on the other person's time. For example, don't schedule a time when you know the other person will be consumed with end of month processing or before a big deadline.

Ensure you don't schedule it too far off in the future. The feedback you're seeking should have a reasonable proximity in time to the work or events it relates to.

Think through what you want to ask

To maximise the value of your feedback session, think through the things you want to ask about and how you will ask them in advance. You don't want to be sitting in the session blankly fumbling for the next question to ask or regret afterwards that you didn't ask about a particular thing.

Care in formulating your questions will help to generate more specific feedback. Think through your particular situation, the people you are working with, the work you are doing, and any difficulties you might be facing. The more specific your questions are, the more specific your feedback will be and that makes it easier to define the concrete actions you will take to improve.

Don't limit your questions to the things you think need to improve. Consider your strengths and competencies as well. Just because you think you're good at something doesn't mean it can't improve.

> What did you observe that I could do better when I facilitated the Team meeting on Monday?
>
> What could I do to improve the way I ...?
>
> How can I improve how I support our team?
>
> What more can I do to be better at ...?

One or two general questions can be valuable as well.

> In what ways can I improve my work performance?

And my favourite one of all:

> What can I stop doing or start doing that would make me easier to work with?

Listen

Listen carefully to the feedback you receive. Don't judge what is being offered and try to avoid thinking about what you will say next as the person helping you is speaking.

Our normal thinking mode when in a conversation with someone is to have our next sentence prepared before we speak. This often means that we are preparing that sentence based on something the other person said early in a sentence and we're not really listening very effectively to the rest of what they say.

When receiving feedback, it is important to set aside your own thinking so you can listen without distraction.

Take notes

Note down the feedback you receive. This shows the other person that you value their feedback and are grateful for their time. Recording the feedback you receive also indicates that you are taking it seriously and will act on it.

Clarify the feedback so you're sure what they're saying

Ask clarifying questions to ensure you're hearing what the other person is trying to relay to you.

Play back what you've heard, paraphrasing or reframing the points made so you can confirm that you heard it correctly and understood the intent.

Suggest actions you might take relating to a point of feedback and propose ways to measure that the action is actually creating the improvement being recommended.

Be grateful

Thank the person who has helped you by providing feedback.

You may have received feedback that can improve your performance in ways that will be beneficial throughout the rest of your life. The contribution that person has made to your life and the gift they have given you by sharing their feedback may be beyond measure.

Even if you are not sure how important the feedback is or how helpful the improvements will be, thank the other person as if their feedback is immensely valuable. Even if the feedback you received today is not all that useful, you have had another opportunity to receive feedback that will hopefully allow you to make even the smallest of beneficial adjustments.

Activity

Explicitly asking for feedback is a fantastic thing to do that can provide insights about ways you might improve that you could not find on your own.

How you go about asking for feedback has a huge impact on the feedback you receive.

Follow the steps above and set up a structured feedback session with someone you trust who is in a position to provide you with feedback.

Schedule it now.

Block out some time for yourself in your calendar before you meet to prepare your questions.

CHAPTER 11

You Can't See the Label From Inside the Jar

Whether you are looking to improve yourself, your team or your organisation, you will struggle to see the whole system when you are a part of it.

This is largely because any human system is immensely complex and seeing the interplay between all the elements of the system involves being able to assess the entire system honestly and dispassionately.

Regardless of the size of the system, be it an organisation with thousands of staff or just yourself, you need to make sense of the values, beliefs, processes, practices, behaviours, and cultures. Trying to see the system from within will always gloss over important elements that are 'just how it is' while elevating the importance of elements that appear as 'obvious'.

When assessing a system you are a part of, there are two ways you can get an external view so you can see the label.

1. Get outside the jar
2. Hold up a mirror

Get outside the jar

Getting outside the jar involves taking a viewpoint other than the one you usually take. This can be extremely difficult, but it is always rewarding in the insights it provides.

The viewpoint from outside the jar needs you to be able to put aside your own biases and ask yourself some challenging questions. Some of these questions will relate to the entire system while some are best applied to each element of the system.

Thinking of your overall system as the *people*, the *processes* and the *tools* means you will be looking at: the culture in the system and how you and the people around you interact with each other and how you go about your activities.

The examination of what is outside the jar is greatly supported by having clarity on the outcomes the system is endeavouring to create. Every system has outcomes and every individual part of that system has outcomes. Most systems aren't explicit about the outcomes they seek and this leads to a focus on outputs. Without explicit outcomes, the system will continue to produce outputs but the outcome those outputs produce may not be as valuable and could even be undesirable.

If you don't have compelling outcomes that are explicitly defined in a way that provides clarity to everyone who is a part of your system, then is becomes very difficult to assess the parts of the system. Is a process optimised for providing the most valuable outcomes? Are behaviours aligned to valuable outcomes? Are people interacting in ways that produce value for the people as well as for the outcomes?

When you're looking at the system from outside and you have at least some idea of the outcomes sought, you can start to examine whether elements of culture, practices or tools are best suiting the system in ways that will reduce your natural cognitive bias (you won't be able to eliminate cognitive bias, but you can reduce its impacts.)

When you break the overall system down into its constituent elements, look for things that help you have visibility of the overall flow of valuable outcomes, areas of culture that increase or decrease intrinsic motivation, behaviours that enhance collaboration or create silos, environmental elements that support empowerment or create subservience, things that bring flow or create resistance.

For each element of the system as well as the overall system, ask yourself:

- What can I measure that will increase transparency or visibility?
- Does this support the people in the system?

- Is there a simpler way?
- How could I uplift my capability?
- Could this be done faster?
- What would this look like to a <insert customer, friend, partner>?
- What would the headline look like in the media?
- How would a <insert random profession, like chef, or archaeologist> deal with this?
- What would happen if we stopped doing this all together?
- How can I improve the quality?
- Could this be automated?
- What steps could be eliminated?
- Is this genuinely valuable?
- Are there areas of capability lacking?

These questions are just thought provokers to help get you going in your investigation. Once you start examining your system with some level of objectivity, other questions will arise. Allow yourself to explore the system organically, bringing together ideas from other professions, products, or processes.

Hold up a mirror

In order to hold up a mirror to your jar to enable you to see the label on the outside, you need to get support from someone outside the jar.

This might be a life coach if you are evaluating your personal system, or a business coach or agile coach if you are evaluating your work or your Team.

Often someone outside the system will see the elements of the system that are constrained or otherwise sub-optimised more clearly.

The person outside the jar who will hold up the mirror for you will perform the same investigation that you would from inside the jar, except that they will not be hampered by the same cognitive biases that you would have – and they will more readily examine the elements of your system that you may not think to look into because they are 'how it has always been'.

Inside or outside

Whether you are looking at your system from the inside with your mind as open as possible or you're seeking support from someone outside the system, the outcomes are similar. What will you do differently?

While the person helping from the outside can bring more clarity due to having less cognitive bias, both approaches will lead to a set of observations about things within your system that could be improved.

Having made your observations, the most important thing becomes: what will you do about them?

In order to know which of the elements identified will be the most valuable to improve, you need to understand the root cause behind each element.

Many times, attempting to change the part of the system that you have observed as being sub-optimised is difficult and fraught with danger. Understanding the root cause behind the dysfunction will very often provide an insight into something very small that can be changed.

Case Study:

One team I worked with was in a constant struggle with strong personalities actively competing with each other. Constant bickering and aggressive behaviours were holding them back from achieving their goals and they had produced very little value for a long time.

Over time, the culture of the team devolved into one of open warfare visible as seemingly childish behaviours. Certain people in the team would avoid each other or oppose each other's suggestions in meetings simply to be obstructive.

Previous leaders had tried to intervene at the level of the behaviours themselves, trying to get the opposing parties together to work through their difficulties, working with individuals to coach them on how they might work more collaboratively, but nothing they tried had any impact on the underlying problems and there were such high levels of stress and dissatisfaction that there was a 20% attrition rate.

Taking the view from outside the jar exposed the fact that people had individual objectives that were not aligned. They were working on the same team but operating as separate parts of the system going in different directions, resulting in the whole Team going nowhere.

All we needed to do was reset the objectives. Instead of individual objectives with the necessary individual performance management within a system optimised for individual utilisation, we established a single team objective with performance management aimed at the overall effectiveness of the team for delivery towards that objective.

With the system optimised for team effectiveness, we immediately saw a change in the behaviours and culture within the team.

Collaboration improved and the focus shifted from outputs to outcomes. The pace of delivery tripled and quality improved. Most satisfying of all, the mood of the Team was noticeably uplifted. People were smiling more, happier to come to work, sick days reduced to almost zero and attrition became zero.

Activity

Create a view of the label on your jar.

Choose something you can do to get visibility of the jar you're in and do it.

Will you choose to get outside the jar and reflect on the viewpoint of those around you to consider how their viewpoint might provide new insights? If so, what scope will you apply it to? Which jar will you reflect on? Yourself? Your team?

Will you choose to hold up a mirror and get direct feedback from those who are outside the jar? Again, what scope will you ask for feedback on. Yourself, your team or something else?

It's easier to reflect on the team space or to get feedback on the team. It takes courage to apply these to the personal level.

Approach	Scope	What will you do?
☐ Get outside the jar ☐ Hold up a mirror		

Writing it down is one thing. Now go and do it!

What did you learn?

What will you do differently as a result of that learning?

Things I learnt	Things I will do differently

Summary – Being Agile

In this section, we've covered an overview of agile and being an agile individual.

What is agile?

Agile is a mindset and a way of being. It is not a framework because it doesn't give you a frame within which you do your work. It is not a methodology because it doesn't give you methods.

A Venn Diagram of Agile

We looked at the three imperatives: doing the right thing, doing the thing right, and doing it in short iterations so you can learn. We looked at the importance of seeking balance between the three and concluded with an exercise where you plotted your own work and came up with something you can do to move your work closer to the centre so the three imperatives are closer to being in balance.

Purpose

The value and importance of having a personal purpose in helping you to select the work that will align with your 'why' and in helping you to go about that work in a way that makes it intrinsically motivating.

The activity for the purpose chapter was a simplified approach to defining your own personal purpose statement.

Flow

We discussed the meaning of flow and what it is like to be in a state of flow before describing how to know when you're in a flow state and some ways to choose the work that you're doing to help you achieve it more often along with ways to go about the work to increase your chances of slipping into a flow state.

In the flow state activity, you rated the things that give you joy based on how much they put you in a state of flow, followed by defining ways to bring more of those things into your life.

SUMMARY - BEING AGILE

Change

The agile individual not only accepts that change is inevitable, they are an agent for bringing about good change.

Things always turn out best for the person who makes the most out of the way things turn out. The agile individual is not fixed in any of their ways of working or being and is able to adapt to their circumstances.

We explored the idea of bringing about positive change through the Dream Team case study, before completing an activity to define a positive change in a single step in your work process.

The change chapter also delved into adaptability and how to enable dealing with change when you are not the instigator of it by being able to adapt to circumstances as they emerge. The adaptability activity encouraged you to look at the ideas you hold to be true and what the impact would be if they turned out to not be true.

You didn't decide what to do if your beliefs turn out to be based on something that isn't true, but having thought through those beliefs being challenged you are already in a better position to adapt should you need to.

Learning or Winning

We looked at the difference between learning and winning and how an agile individual focuses their efforts on learning over winning in the short term, because they know that continuously improving themselves and their capability is what it takes to win in the long term.

In the activity at the end of the Learning or Winning chapter, you reflected on how you might change your viewpoint to change your outcomes.

You redefined the big things you're working on as learning opportunities so you can increase your learning and create success at having learned something regardless of the outcome of the project.

You then did the same with the challenges you're facing, changing the way you see them from being negative things that are getting in your way to being positive things that will help you to grow.

Growth is Not Comfortable

The growth chapter introduced the idea that we tend to stay in our comfort zones which eliminates opportunities to grow. The activity for this chapter encouraged you to find your discomfort zone by identifying something you have been skilfully avoiding, deciding on one small thing you can do to get you closer to resolving that and committing to a date by when you will do it.

Making Sense

We discussed how the brain makes sense of the world and how it prioritises survival, conservation of energy and building habits over deep thinking and that it takes effort to apply thinking to situations, especially when they are stressful

In the activity you identified stressors you have experienced and how your default feelings and thoughts brought about a result. You then invested the effort to apply different thinking and a different perspective and consider what that would mean for your feeling and thinking and how that can create a different result.

Cognitive Biases

We looked at several cognitive biases, their impacts on how we operate and ways to deal with them.

With the focus on confirmation bias, egocentric bias and group think we concluded the chapter by defining something concrete you will do in the next week to deal with bias in yourself and in others.

Feedback

Feedback is a loving gift that helps you to improve.

Feedback can provide clarity on something that needs to change and brings opportunities to improve. In this chapter we went through a structured approach to seeking and receiving feedback with an activity where you scheduled a structured feedback session with someone you trust.

You Can't See the Label From Inside the Jar

We're all operating within systems that we become a part of in ways that make it difficult to see what is really happening within the system.

Two approaches to assessing the system you inhabit were discussed. Opening your mind to a view from outside the system and asking a trusted advisor from outside the system to hold up a mirror. Both approaches aim to provide you with a view of the system that exposes opportunities to improve.

You set in motion an activity to create a view from outside the system you're inhabiting, make sure you follow up by acting on the information that emerges.

SECTION 2
DOING AGILE

BE AGILE

There is a way to do it better — find it!

—Thomas A. Edison

***

There is nothing so useless as doing efficiently that which should not be done at all.

—Peter Drucker

***

Planning is everything.
Plans are nothing.

—Field Marshal Helmuth von Moltke

***

Perfect is the enemy of done.

—Catherine Carrigan

***

DOING AGILE

The agile individual practices agile ways of working.

Doing agile involves approaching work in ways that allow you to get feedback faster by delivering value in smaller pieces. The shorter feedback loop gives you opportunities to quickly test ideas and change direction if you find that the idea needs to adapt.

There is no point whatsoever in going faster if you're going in the wrong direction, so one of the underlying ideas in working in agile ways is to get information as often as possible about whether the goal you're heading towards is still valid and whether the work you're doing is actually going to get you there.

You'll hear terms used like, "Test and learn," or, "Safe to fail experiment," or, "Fail fast," that capture the idea of trying something out and seeing what happens with the intent of learning. In a complex world that is changing faster every day, learning about what is really important is more valuable than delivering something perfect.

In this section we cover:

- Setting Goals
- Backlogs
- Estimation
- Prioritisation
- Experimentation
- Make Work Visible
- Incremental and Iterative
- Outcome Over Output

BE AGILE

- Timeboxing
- Stop Starting and Start Finishing
- Meaningful Metrics and How to Use Them
- Fail Fast
- Continuous Improvement and Compounding Interest
- Deliberate Practice

CHAPTER 1
Setting Goals

An agile individual sets goals that represent valuable outcomes and works towards them iteratively and incrementally. They progress by building up small improvements in short bursts that contribute to those goals.

Working iteratively and incrementally towards valuable outcomes involves first of all knowing what your valuable outcomes are.

Without meaningful goals in place, your small regular achievements may not be adding up to the same longer-term result and may, in fact, be working in opposition to each other.

Setting goals involves deciding what your 'north star' is. What

> *SETTING GOALS IS THE FIRST STEP IN TURNING THE INVISIBLE INTO THE VISIBLE.*
> *Tony Robbins*

is the result that you want all your smaller achievements to work towards?

That might not be so easy. It is not always immediately obvious what your longer-term purpose should be, what will motivate you to get out of bed in the morning, or what will provide your life with meaning.

If you google "goal setting", most of what you will find is about how your goals should be SMART, (**S**pecific, **M**easurable, **A**chievable, (or aspirational,) **R**elevant, and **T**ime bound.) That is all well and good (your goals should have all those ingredients,) but it doesn't help you determine *which* goals to set.

Setting goals for things you want to get is easy: if there is something you really want, then it naturally lends itself to forming a goal around it and it is relatively simple to make it a SMART goal. If for example, you really want to own your own home, you might set a goal like this:

> I will own a 3 bedroom home in <suburb> with a large back yard and parking for 2 cars by 31 December 2022.

That works fine for a SMART goal – it is specific enough to know exactly what sort of house you want, it is measurable in that you will own the house or not, you will need to adjust your financial situation to make it achievable, it is relevant because it is the thing you really want, and by setting a date you have made it time-bound.

But what if there is no specific thing that you want to get? How do you go about setting goals that will actually have any meaning for you? A SMART goal that does not get you feeling excited enough to motivate you to do more than you're already doing today is not so smart.

Goals that represent who you want to become or how you want to contribute to the world will always be more motivating than those about something you want to receive. *Giving* contributes much more to your mental and emotional wellbeing than receiving does.

Goals that align with your values and enable your growth will be the goals that get you out of bed in the morning.

Goals that can be broken down into smaller targets make it easier to see your progress towards your goals. This will bring a sense of achievement that helps motivate you to keep going and builds resilience to help you push through the difficult times.

So how do you go about setting goals that align to your values, enable your growth and can be broken down to smaller achievements?

My personal favourite way to establish goals is the **narrative approach**. I've coached many individuals in using it to design their personal goals and facilitated many large and small groups in applying it to bigger pieces of work.

The narrative approach to goal setting works beautifully in creating personal goals, but it is equally effective at setting the purpose for an organisation, the vision for a product or specific outcomes for a project.

The beauty of the narrative approach to goal setting is that it results in goals that are much more compelling and motivating than any of the formulaic approaches I have seen. Sure, the ease with which you can complete a formula makes it attractive, and you don't need to apply too much thought or imagination to a formula, but the outcome is far less valuable.

You can use the narrative approach to goal setting on your own when setting personal goals, but you will find it much better if you get the support of a coach or friend to facilitate for you. The simplification and alignment that comes from an effective facilitator will allow you to focus on the story as the facilitator frames the activity and captures the essence of your stories, making it easier to distil the goals that emerge at the end.

The narrative approach has 10 major steps to work through:

1. Establish your values
2. Define your customer(s)

SETTING GOALS

3. What problems do your customers have?
4. Recount your past successes
5. Tell your future stories
6. Extract impacts and contributions
7. Distil your goals
8. Break down your goals
9. Establish success measures and feedback loops
10. Get on with it

You don't necessarily need to complete them all, and you don't have to give them all the same investment. Choose for yourself how much to put into each step. For example, you may feel that the customer in your personal goals is yourself and decide not to put time into that step.

Establish your values

What do you value?

This sounds like a simple question, just 4 words, but it is not as easy as it sounds. This is one of the things a facilitator will really help you with.

Your values are those things that matter to you in how you live and work and how you relate to others.

When everything you do aligns to your values, you get a deep-seated feeling that things are going in a direction conducive to your being.

When values are used to set priorities, you work within the knowledge that what you are doing is important and valuable.

When priorities are set without concern for your values, you can find yourself working on things that feel like they don't really matter. This will often be the case when your priorities are set by other people. Externally-defined priorities don't often feel natural or aligned to your greater purpose. It might be the nature of your work and may not be something you have a lot of agency over, but if you find that it is the case, applying your values to your personal goals will at least give you control over that part of your life.

This is why identifying your values is of such importance.

To get started with establishing your values, reflect on the highlights in your life. Don't limit your thinking to your work – think through your personal highlights, family life and friends. Finding what matters to you means looking at all aspects of your life.

- Think of a moment when you were really happy.
    - What was happening?
    - What were you doing? Feeling? Thinking?

- Who were you with?
  - When was it? Where was it?
  - What was the cause of your happiness?

- Think of a moment when you were really proud.
  - Was it a significant contribution you had just made?
  - Was it the contribution you made to someone else's success?
  - Did it come after completing a particularly difficult challenge?
  - Was your proud moment shared with others in a group success?

- Think of a moment when you felt really fulfilled.
  - What was it that left you feeling fulfilled?
  - Did others share your feelings of fulfillment?

When you have listed out your personal highlights, think through each experience or event and refine it down to a single word. You might need an intermediary step to first condense a sentence into a short phrase.

Here are some common values words to help you.

BE AGILE

Abstinence
Acceptance
Accountability
Accuracy
Achievement
Adventure
Altruism
Ambition
Approval
Assertiveness
Attractiveness
Balance
Beauty
Being the best
Belief
Belonging
Certainty
Challenge
Cheerfulness
Collaboration
Commitment
Communication
Community
Compassion
Competitiveness
Composure
Confidence
Connection
Consistency
Contentment
Contribution

Control
Cooperation
Correctness
Courage
Courtesy
Creativity
Curiosity
Daring
Debate
Decisiveness
Dedication
Dependability
Determination
Diligence
Discipline
Discovery
Discretion
Diversity
Dynamism
Effectiveness
Efficiency
Elegance
Empathy
Enjoyment
Enthusiasm
Equality
Excellence
Excitement
Experience
Expertise
Exploration

Fairness
Faith
Family
Fidelity
Fitness
Fitting in
Focus
Freedom
Friends
Fun
Generosity
Goodness
Grace
Gratitude
Growth
Happiness
Hard Work
Harmony
Health
Helping
Holiness
Honesty
Honour
Humility
Ideas
Independence
Individuality
Ingenuity
Innovation
Inquisitiveness
Insightfulness

SETTING GOALS

Intelligence	Perseverance	Shrewdness
Interaction	Piety	Simplicity
Introspection	Play	Sincerity
Intuition	Positivity	Skilfulness
Joy	Pragmatism	Soundness
Judgement	Precision	Speed
Justice	Preparedness	Spontaneity
Kindness	Professionalism	Stability
Knowledge	Prudence	Status
Leadership	Quality	Strategic
Learning	Questioning	Strength
Legacy	Quietness	Structure
Liberty	Realism	Success
Logic	Recognition	Support
Love	Reliability	Teamwork
Loyalty	Relationships	Tenacity
Mastery	Resourcefulness	Temperance
Meaning	Respect	Thankfulness
Merit	Responsibility	Thoughtfulness
Modesty	Restraint	Timeliness
Novelty	Results	Tolerance
Obedience	Rigour	Travel
Openness	Safety	Trust
Optimism	Sanity	Truth
Order	Security	Understanding
Originality	Self-actualisation	Unity
Partnership	Selflessness	Usefulness
Passion	Self-reliance	Vision
Patience	Sensitivity	Vitality
Patriotism	Serenity	Wellbeing
Perfection	Service	Winning

Which of the values listed resonates with you when you think about it?

Create your list of values then refine it down to no more than a dozen or so. A lot of values in the list are very similar with only subtle differences between them. This is intentional: while you probably connect with all of the similar values, you'll need to choose the one that best describes what you feel when you consider that value.

When you have your values listed, prioritise them so you can identify the top 3 or 4. Think about each value in your list. Which ones generate the strongest feelings for you? Don't underestimate the value of this step, and don't try to have more than one value at equal priority. Ranking them into a single prioritised list will force you to think through what you really value at a deeper level than if you simply say, "I value both of these things equally."

If you're struggling to choose one value over another, put them into the context of a choice that includes both values. For example, if you value Teamwork and Innovation, would you rather be on a Team that works brilliantly together but is not doing anything innovative, or on a Team that struggles to work together but is creating something completely innovative? Ask yourself how you would feel if you could only have one of them. Which would it be?

Now reflect on your top 3 or 4 values. How do they make you feel? Would you be comfortable sharing them with others?

With your values identified, you can use them in your decision making and in setting you goals. When your goals and decisions align with your values, you will find a deep sense of alignment with what you are doing, even if it is difficult or challenging. With your values clearly articulated, you can make the hard decisions and take on the difficult challenges.

Define your customer(s)

Defining your customers for your personal goals is subtly different than how you would go about it for a business or product perspective.

You're less interested in demographics for your personal goals than you would be in a business sense because this is not as much about marketing to them as it is about defining goals that will resonate with you and help you to choose work that is intrinsically motivating. In the case of personal goals, you are often your own customer.

The natural thought is that you serve your boss, or whoever employed you, but this will limit your thinking and reduce your understanding of how you bring value to the world. Your company has employed you to do a job, but it wants you to deliver that value from that job to customers or colleagues.

Consider how you will be valuable to them. Clarity over who you serve allows you to explore what problems they have and how your actions and ideas can solve those problems.

What problems do your customers have?

Knowing what problems you solve for those you serve helps you determine how you will apply your values.

The better you understand the problems you will be solving, the more likely you will be able to find simple and effective solutions. Clarity on the problem being solved changes the way you think about your work from a focus on completing tasks to providing an outcome.

- What benefit will people receive?
- What will you help people achieve?
- What pain will you relieve?

Thinking about the problem you solve makes the outcome more compelling and motivating than thinking about how you solve it. The outcome matters to people and that makes it matter more to you.

If, for example, you are a security guard, you could think about the way you solve the problems you have been hired to solve, but you'll think about it differently if you think about the outcomes you create for people.

In the example above, you might be hired to maintain security and your KPIs could be based on having no security breaches. That's great and you have every opportunity to do a good job and perform well. But the perspective of seeing your goal as creating a safe and secure work environment for everyone who works at your company so they can enjoy a harmonious workplace might be more compelling and will allow you to find innovative ways to deliver even more value.

Understanding that those you serve are your work colleagues rather than your boss and the way you serve them is by creating harmony, safety and security doesn't change the fact that the way you are measured is still about preventing security breaches, but it might change the way you go about it. You might be more likely to greet colleagues with a smile and to help out in areas beyond the basics of the job.

Recount your past successes

With your list of values, an understanding of who you serve and the problems you solve for them, your next step is to reflect on your successes.

When we think about our successes, we usually think about the times we achieved something recognised by our employer or a community of some sort, but that's not what we're looking for here. For this step in the goal setting exercise, recount the times when you operated in concert with your values to solve the problem or provide a benefit for the customers you identified.

Write them down. Writing your success stories on paper forces you to think through the wording as well as the event. You'll consider them more deeply and include more of the important details if you write them down as opposed to just thinking about them.

Tell your future stories

Putting yourself in the shoes of those you serve, set your mind to the future.

What stories would those people share about the outcomes of what you have done? If they were at a barbeque with friends having just received the benefit of what you do or had their problems solved by you, what story would they tell?

What story would you want them to tell?

Imagine them telling their story and sharing how your work contributed to their lives. What are the details? What problem did you solve? What benefit did you create for them? What impact did it have on their lives to have that problem solved or benefit realised?

Extract impacts and contributions

Now highlight or underline the words and phrases that represent the details where you made a contribution to the lives of those you serve or had some positive impact on them in each of the past success stories and future imagined stories.

SETTING GOALS

Create a new list of the impact and contribution words and phrases from both sets of stories.

Group similar impacts and contributions together. If there is a dominant theme in a group, give it a name that represents the theme.

You now have a list of your impacts or contributions to those you serve, combined with the impacts and contributions you want to have in the future.

Mull over this list for a few minutes.

- What does it mean to you to make those contributions?
- How do you feel about the impact you have had or want to have?
- Are there any synonyms that give a word or group in your list more resonance?

Distil your goals

This is the point where you turn all the previous steps into one or two future-oriented statements that are compelling and motivating.

Try to make it SMART (Specific, Measurable, Aspirational, Realistic, Timebound,) but don't let that be the dominant thing in writing your goal. If it is not easily measured for example, then you can refine that part of it later. The most important thing about your goal is that it inspires you.

Let's take a look at an example.

Imagine someone going through this goal setting exercise who is a Scrum Master in their mid 20s. They are reasonably new to their role, but they're already enjoying it and they're keen to learn more.

Our imaginary Scrum Master has chosen Community, Learning and Helping as their top 3 values.

They have defined a Scrum Master Meetup group they belong to as a customer. They have received a lot of learning from this Meetup group and they're keen to help others learn too.

The problems they've defined for their customer are that most of the Meetup group participants are new to their role, uncertain of what they should learn or how to access learning opportunities.

Among their past success stories, they recall an experience when they facilitated a learning game at the Meetup that helped participants to understand relative vs absolute estimation. The impact and contribution created by this experience included people gaining clarity in why relative estimation is important, knowledge of how to go about it and increased confidence in their role.

Our Scrum Master's future success stories include a presentation at a major international agile conference about how Scrum

SETTING GOALS

Masters should not solve their team's problems so the team can learn to solve their problems themselves. The contribution and impact of this presentation includes 'aha' moments for the audience as they learn that Scrum Masters can remove impediments by empowering their teams rather than solving their problems.

They decide on setting a goal to deliver that speech at the biggest agile conference in their home city.

In order to make it SMART, they define their goal as:

> "I will deliver a presentation about Scrum Masters empowering their teams at Agile Australia in Sydney 2023"

Their goal is specific, measurable, aspirational, realistic and timely. It will be quite a challenge to achieve this, but it also inspires them to do more and become more.

When you have a SMART goal that matters to you, convert it into the present tense and preface it with gratitude.

It will sound crazy at first, but writing your goal as if you're grateful for already having it activates your subconscious mind to bring it to you.

Have you ever noticed how people who already have plenty of money seem to be the ones who get the most? Have you noticed that when you've bought a new car you suddenly see lots of that make, model and colour car?

Tricking your subconscious into thinking you already have achieved the outcome of your goal puts it into a thinking track that the outcome exists and is plentiful enough for you to get one. It will notice opportunities to bring that thing to you more readily when it believes it is abundant.

Have you ever noticed that those who have the least, struggle to get any more? People who repeatedly say, "I can't afford …," make it true because they are telling their subconscious mind that they don't have enough and there is not enough in the universe.

Having your goal in your mind as something you don't have puts it in the realm of things you lack. Clearly there is not enough in the universe, or you'd have one.

Now write out your goals on paper. Write them large and as beautifully as you can. Use colour, draw pictures or diagrams, add photos, make it stand out. Create a few copies.

Stick your goals on the fridge, on the wall next to your bed, beside your front door, or next to your bathroom mirror. Put them up where you will see them frequently throughout the day.

Break down your goals

With goals staring you in the face every day that are aspirational, motivating, aligned with your values, and written as if you are

SETTING GOALS

grateful for already having them, you are much more likely to achieve them. However, having the goals is not enough. You also need to do something towards achieving them.

There is no magic in the world that will make those outcomes happen without investing time, effort and resources. You need to invest of yourself in order to bring about change in yourself.

Break your goals down into the different horizons.

The timebound aspect of your goal may be a year away. That's your destination. What are the milestones in your journey towards that destination? These become the targets you need to hit along the way in order to achieve your goal within the specified timeframe.

If the milestones are several months apart, continue to break them down until you have concrete objectives that are roughly a month or so apart. Don't worry too much about those that are way off into the future. The ones that are coming up in the next few months are the ones to focus on.

Next, consider what you need to do to achieve the first few of those monthly objectives. Because it is only a month away, it shouldn't be too difficult to define what needs to be done in order to meet the objective.

Our imaginary Scrum Master who set their goal to speak at Agile Australia might break their goal down into a series of milestones based on presentations given at increasingly larger events.

Their first event might be their own Meetup Group, so that gives them something much smaller that will give them the experience and confidence they need to proceed to the next step.

Establish success measures and feedback loops

The final step is to figure out how you will measure success and how you can get feedback on the activities that will create the objectives. With clarity on what you need to do to achieve your first few monthly objectives, putting success measures and feedback loops in place greatly improves your chances of getting there.

In a study of the motivational effect of feedback on performance published in the Journal of Applied Psychology in 1978, 80 families were given goals to reduce their electricity consumption with another 20 families included as a control group.

Half of the families were given an aspirational goal of reducing their electricity consumption by 20% and the other half were given a comparatively easy goal of reducing it by 5%. Half of each of those groups were provided with feedback 3 times a week on how they were going.

Exactly as predicted, the 20 families that had the aspirational goal and received regular feedback performed the best, with up to 25% reduction in their electricity consumption. Not all of them achieved the desired 20% reduction – the lowest improvement was only

SETTING GOALS

13% – but all of them achieved better results than the families with the easy goal or the control group, and the average result was significantly higher than the families that didn't get feedback.

The study gives us an example of a simple success measure (the rate of decrease in electricity consumption,) and a feedback loop (review the success measure three times a week.) The two together increased motivation and helped the families to stick with the activities that contributed to their goal.

Feedback doesn't tell you what to do. It tells you about something you've already done. If you tried something different and the feedback suggested it worked, you might decide to do more of it – but the feedback comes after the doing, not before.

While feedback doesn't help you know what to do, it does motivate you to try harder and stick with something difficult for longer.

Our imaginary Scrum Master, whose goal is to speak at Agile Australia, might implement 2 feedback loops.

The first could be a feedback poster audience members stick Post-It® Notes with categories of how they felt and whether they learned anything.

The other feedback loop might be to seek feedback directly from event organisers around how they found the experience of working together and what they might do differently to be easier to work with.

Get on with it

You now have values-based goals and clarity over who it is that you serve, along with the problems that you solve for them. You've reflected on your past successes and told the stories you want your customers to tell after they benefit from what you do. From those past and future stories, you extracted the impact and contribution that you've had or want to have and used those to define clear long-term goals.

You've broken your long-term goals into near horizons of a month or so and you know how you will get feedback on whether or not those short-term goals are working towards your overarching goals.

The only thing left to do is to get on with it.

- What do you need to do this month?
- How will you measure that it is working?
- How will you collect feedback?

Activity

Using the Goal Canvas on the next page, apply the narrative approach to establish your own goals and a plan for how you will achieve them.

SETTING GOALS

You may need to use additional pieces of paper for working out your values and listing the impacts and contributions from your past and future stories before you enter the resulting lists into the canvas.

1. Establish your values
2. Define your customer(s)
3. What problems do your customers have?
4. Recount your past successes
5. Tell your future stories
6. Extract impacts and contributions
7. Distil your goals
8. Break down your goals
9. Establish success measures and feedback loops
10. Get on with it

You can download an editable goal canvas at https://www.terryhaayema.com/templates

BE AGILE

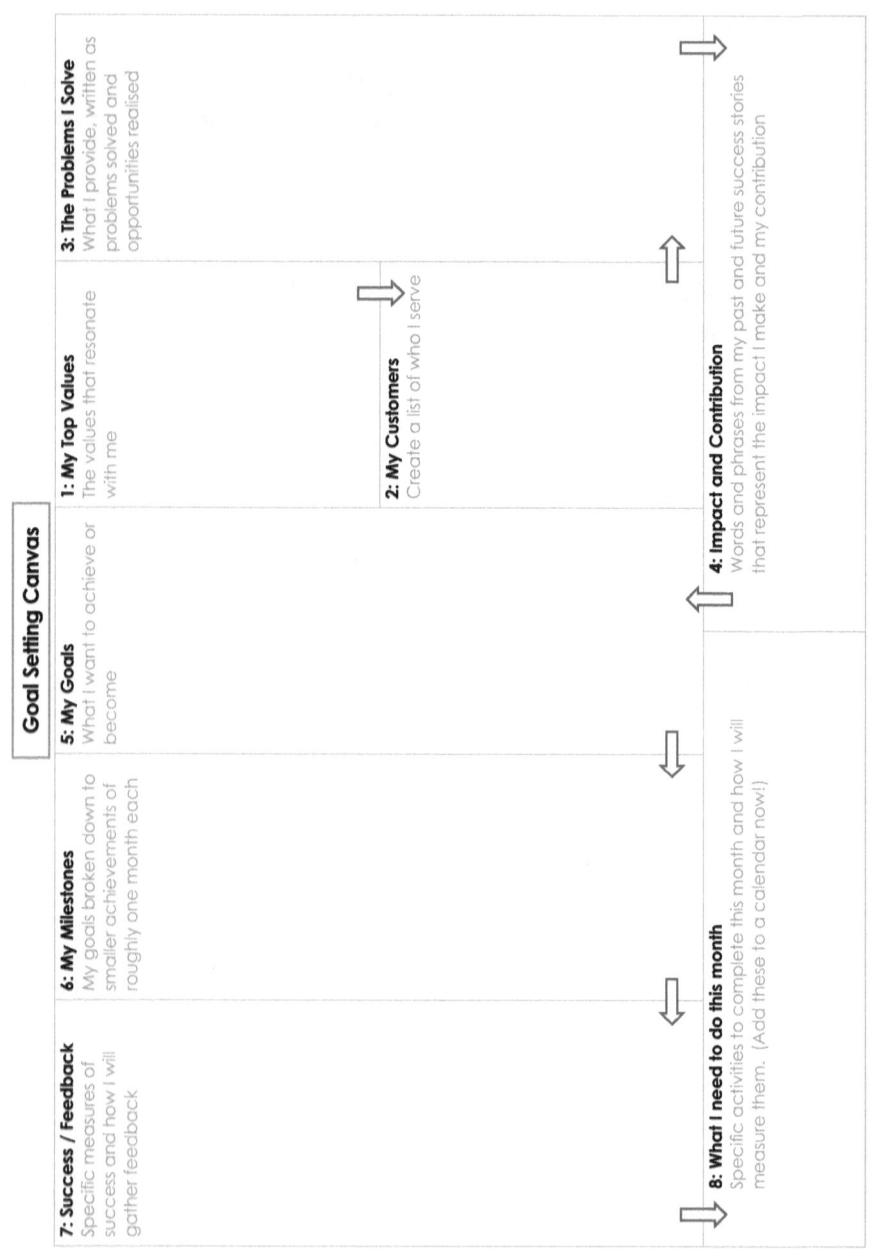

CHAPTER 2

BACKLOGS

An agile individual makes their work visible in a list that allows them to ensure they are always working on the most important and most valuable things.

A backlog is a lot like a task list. It is simply a way to make all the things you know you need to do visible so you can organise it and then get on with the most valuable things.

The difference between a backlog and a task list is that you consciously apply a lens of priority and size across your backlog all the time.

There are many ways to think about your backlog. In the Scrum Framework it is described as a Product Backlog, suggesting that all the items contained within it belong to maintenance and improvement of a single product.

That might work for a software team, but from the perspective of an agile individual, creating a backlog for each of the areas within which you want to work will only add complexity and make it hard to choose what you should be working on next.

For the agile individual, the backlog we will describe belongs to the group that will deliver the value it describes. So if it is your own backlog, you might call it your personal backlog, if it belongs to a team, you'd call it the team backlog. That way it can hold all the work that needs to be done even if it is across multiple products or areas of value.

The backbone of your backlog should be outcomes, not tasks. Knowing what the outcome is will be much more valuable than knowing what the work is when it comes time to prioritise your backlog.

Your backlog should never get too long. If work is arriving faster than you can complete it, your backlog will continue to get longer and longer over time until you are keeping track of things that were asked for months ago. If you ever do get around to doing them, it will be a long time after they were requested. That's not very agile.

> IT'S ONLY BY SAYING "NO" THAT YOU CAN CONCENTRATE ON THE THINGS THAT ARE REALLY IMPORTANT.
> Steve Jobs

Your backlog should also include the detail of what must be done. The level of detail should be relative to the priority of the item.

If something is high priority, then it should have sufficient detail to know exactly what needs to be done. If it is lower priority, you might just record what the outcome is and leave it at that for now. You will learn more about the lower priority items before you get to them, so any work you do now to refine the details might be wasted.

Your backlog should be sorted in order of priority with the most important things at the top and the least important things at the bottom.

Start with the vision

When you start to prepare your backlog, you want to know that the outcomes you're defining are the most important things that contribute to where you want to go, not just the things that are being asked of you.

See the section on "Purpose" for details in establishing your personal purpose. This will help you to know where you want to go and allow you to define outcomes that will contribute towards it.

List the outcomes

When you have the purpose or vision clearly at the front of your mind you can start to list out the outcomes that will get you closer to your vision or express your purpose.

Be sure to write these as outcomes, not tasks. What is it that you or your customers are going to get out of it?

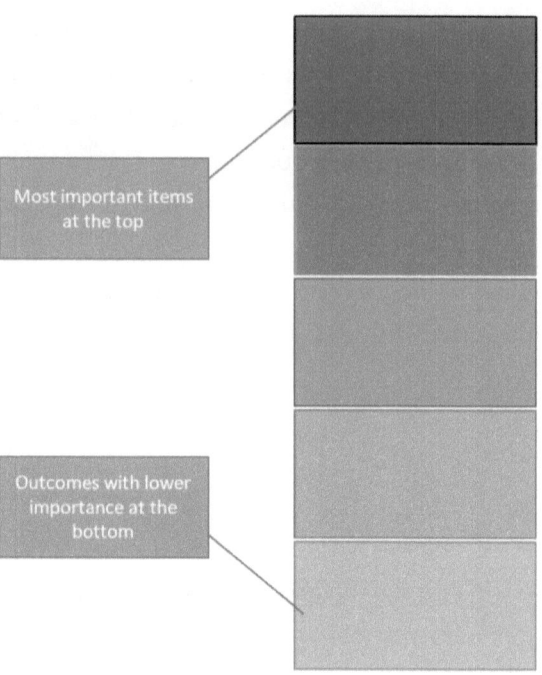

Listing an item as a piece of work removes a lot of flexibility in how you go about delivering it. If it is defined as an outcome, you may find that a really simple way to create the outcome emerges that involves a lot less effort than the task you would have defined.

Prioritise the outcomes based on a combination of how valuable they are and how much effort they would require. See the section on Prioritisation for more details on prioritising based on value and effort.

Break down the most important items

With a prioritised list of outcomes, you can break down the highest priority items into small simple things to deliver the outcome.

BACKLOGS

We don't want to get bogged down in something big, working to complete it before getting feedback and learning. Any number of things can change before we get it done and that change might invalidate the approach we took.

Rather than working on something big and important, the agile individual works on something small that contributes to the big important thing, so they can finish the small thing and get some feedback.

Each time you complete a small thing, you check that you're still going in the right direction, the thing you're striving for is still valuable, and your understanding of what needs to be done is correct.

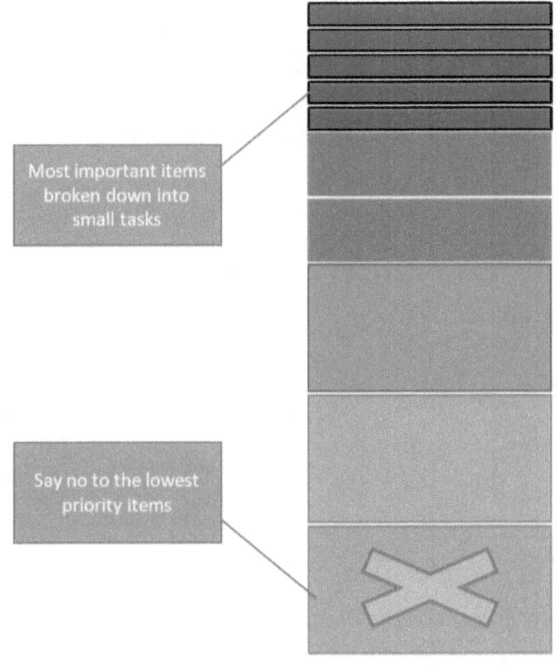

That way, if something does change before you finish the big thing, you can adjust. It is much easier to adjust after a few small things than it is to adjust after finishing the entirety of a big thing.

If you misunderstood what was needed, you will find that out after handing over the first few small things. This is much easier to deal with than finding out you are going in the wrong direction after completely completing the entire big thing.

When you know the smaller tasks you need to deliver, you can now prioritise them. Even though they each contribute to the big important outcome that is your highest priority, they may not all be high priority. You will always find that there are aspects of an important thing that are not as important as others.

If only it could be so simple

As with most things in life, it is never as simple as it seems.

If you're lucky, you can prioritise your outcomes, break the most important ones into smaller bite-sized pieces, prioritise those bite-sized pieces and then simply get on with the highest priority item.

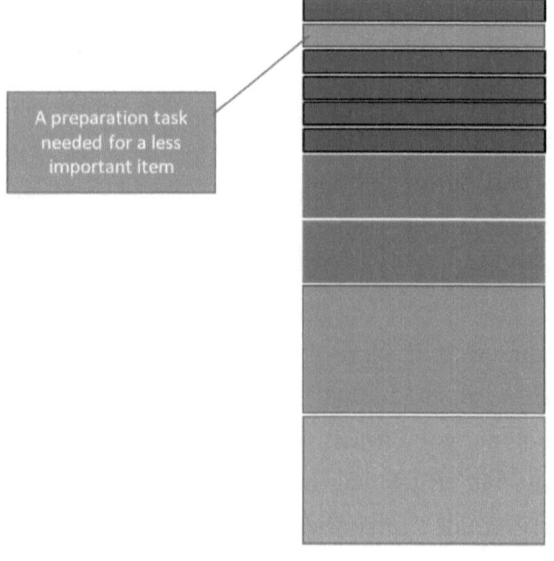

A preparation task needed for a less important item

BACKLOGS

Quite possibly, there will be reasons why you need to interweave items in your backlog from a lower priority outcome amongst the tasks for your highest priority outcome.

To give you an example of this, imagine you are renovating your house. You might determine that the highest priority is being able to bathe in a more modern setting and you've identified your bathroom as the first of your big items to work on.

Breaking down the work of renovating your bathroom, you arrive at a number of smaller tasks, each one a few days or so of work, and you organise them into a natural priority too.

Looking down the list of outcomes, you see that there is one further down around being able to cook in a modern kitchen with easy access to fabulous tools and equipment. One of the items you want to include in the kitchen is a wonderful oven that needs to be shipped from Italy and it will take 6 months to arrive. If you wait until you are working on the kitchen outcome to place the order, then the oven will arrive too late and you will be living without a kitchen for a long time while you wait for your oven.

If you do have preparatory tasks for future outcomes, you might need to include them within the tasks of higher priority outcomes, so you don't get slowed down when you get to them.

Be careful with this though, if you change your mind and decide not to renovate your kitchen, you might get stuck with an expensive Italian oven that you have no use for.

Additionally, you might find that a task for the bathroom (i.e. laying pipes) influences a task of a lower priority (i.e. reviewing plumbing in the kitchen). Because these tasks are linked, it can be beneficial to approach them together at the same time.

Continually reviewing your backlog as you progress will make it easier to spot these connected tasks.

Get on with it

The next most important thing is to get on with it.

Identify the most important thing to be focusing on, and then break the work down, so you can do the highest priority thing.

Activity

Create a backlog.

You can download an initiative backlog template at https://www.terryhaayema.com/templates

Is there a large objective you're working on? Possibly a project at work, or a personal goal?

Instead of thinking of it as an entire scope or a single goal, break it down into individual outcomes and use those to form a backlog before breaking down the highest priority items so you have something small you can get on with.

First write down the vision, purpose or goal.

Vision, purpose or goal

Next, break that goal down into OUTCOMES that contribute to the overall vision.

Priority	Outcomes that contribute towards the vision, purpose or goal

Now break down the highest priority outcome into small tasks (aim for a few days or less.) Remember to include anything you need to do for later outcomes that needs to be done now. And keep an eye out for related tasks that will be easier to complete together.

Priority	Tasks necessary to deliver the highest priority outcome

CHAPTER 3

ESTIMATION

When you're putting together your backlog of valuable outcomes that contribute to your goals, you'll reach a point where you need to know what you'll be getting, when you'll be getting it, and how much it will cost. This is either because you need to communicate that to the people who have an interest in what you're doing, or because you need to know it yourself. Both are equally important to know!

With industrial era thinking, an enormous effort is invested to provide absolute certainty in estimating what would be delivered in excruciating detail,

> *TO BE UNCERTAIN IS TO BE UNCOMFORTABLE, BUT TO BE CERTAIN IS TO BE RIDICULOUS.*
> *Socrates*

exactly when it would be delivered down to a specific date and exactly how much it would cost in dollars, but no matter how much analysis you do up front, you cannot create certainty. Unexpected events will always crop up and those estimates will always be wrong.

Another aspect of industrial age thinking that gets in the way of being able to provide effective estimates is the desire to force those doing the work into committing to a date by which they will be finished. We believe that by providing detailed requirements, each team or person in a cascading series of activities can tell us how long their piece will take. We then simply add up all the individual estimates to arrive at an overall estimate, add a little contingency and we can commit them to completing by that date.

But life isn't that simple and the work they are doing in delivering a significant outcome is not that simple. If it were, it would be something we've done often enough for it to be routine, and it wouldn't be a significant outcome.

After you begin, complexities and unexpected difficulties will emerge that cannot be foreseen, in part because you are operating at the intersection between multiple systems. Within the system that represents the major outcome you are trying to deliver, there will be complexities. There is also the complexity of scheduling the participants. Some of the people you need may not be available at the times you planned, and as soon as one task goes over time, the rest of the schedule is endangered. And finally, there is the complexity in the human system. People are unpredictable – someone you are depending on to complete a task may resign or become pregnant or fall ill.

ESTIMATION

Add on the simple fact that humans are terrible at estimating how long something will take. If it is something we have done many times before and we know exactly how to do it, then our estimates will be reasonably reliable, but most of the work involved in delivering a significant outcome is not simple and has not been done many times before, so it includes any number of unknown elements.

As I write this passage, I'm 18 months into the 'project' to write a book about individual agility. For example, my initial estimate was 12 months and I'm probably still 6 months away from being ready. That's a 100% variance between the initial estimate and the finished product. That doesn't mean I'm working slowly or that the scope of the work has increased. It is simply that humans are bad at estimating how long something will take.

Part of the reason why people are so bad at estimating using time is that we view the past through rose-tinted glasses. When asked to think about how long something will take, we naturally think about how difficult it was to do something similar in the past – but we forget about the difficulties that occurred, the interruptions that distracted us and the fact that we had to fix certain things after we'd finished.

Another reason time-based estimates end up being wrong is that they are not made by the people who will do the work. I've seen many organisations where the people making the commitment are different to the people who will do the work. Sometimes the people who will do the work are not even employed by the organisation until after the project is funded, the commitments have been made, and the work is about to start. I've even seen leaders make commitments to providing customers with a significant capability within a certain time period, before we even understand the problem, let alone the solution.

At face value, this is more efficient: why would we pay a team of expensive professionals before we are ready for them to do the work?

But defining a major piece of work without the people who will do the work involved in the conversation results in a definition of what will be done that doesn't include anyone thinking, "How would we do that?" The impact on your estimates is that they don't include expected complexities let alone the unexpected ones. With no one who will do the work present when you ask yourself, "What could go wrong?" you cannot include estimates about the things that go wrong when doing this kind of work. The people who will do the work bring a much deeper understanding of delivery risk because they have done this sort of thing before.

> PREDICTION IS VERY DIFFICULT, ESPECIALLY ABOUT THE FUTURE.
> *Niels Bohr*

Additionally, the people who will do the work will be much more engaged, accountable and emotionally invested in commitments they have made themselves than they will be in commitments that were made by others. They will work harder to solve problems and meet deadlines when they have ownership of the commitments made.

Rather than trying to provide certainty, an agile individual is comfortable with ambiguity and understands that the value of estimating is in the way it *informs* your planning, not in the plan itself or clairvoyantly knowing the future or as a mechanism for making commitments.

You might be thinking, "But I still need to make commitments," and that is fair enough. An agile individual still makes commitments; it's just the way they go about making those commitments that differs.

Please hold that thought as we go through this section. Your ability to plan and make commitments will still be there at the end, but you'll have a new way to approach it that avoids the need to pretend certainty and make fake commitments that end up putting people under pressure.

There are a couple of things to go through about how we can provide estimates, make plans and commit to deliverables.

- Understand the Cone of Uncertainty
- Relative Estimation
- Honest forecasts and commitments

BE AGILE

Understand the Cone of Uncertainty

The only point at which you can have complete certainty over exactly what you will have, how long it will take, or how much it will cost is after you finish it.

The further back you are from finishing it, the less certainty you can have simply because the unexpected complexities are yet to emerge.

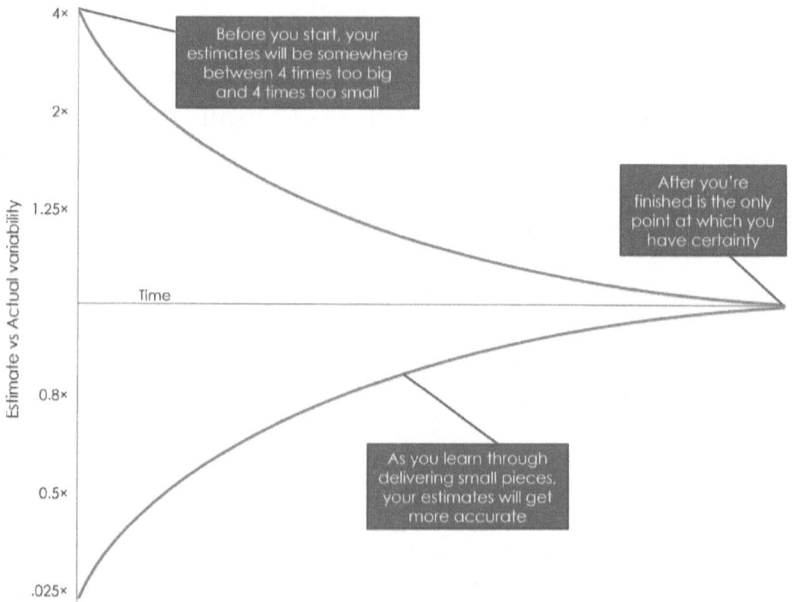

At the very beginning of a major piece of work, you don't know what you don't know and you have yet to learn the lessons that will come each time you do something, each time you solve a problem, and each time you get feedback on something done.

ESTIMATION

Case Study: Automated Payroll System, Queensland Health and IBM

The best example I know of where the Cone of Uncertainty played havoc with a project is the Automated Payroll System launched in 2010 by Queensland Health. Planning and estimation started in 2006 and took more than a year to arrive at the perfect plan. By late 2007, the plan was 'signed off' and IBM were engaged with an estimated cost of $6M AUD. The project was expected to take 6 months.

More than 12 months' worth of planning, estimating, and budgeting was performed without any of the learning that could only be generated by doing the work, facing the challenges and overcoming the difficulties. As a result, none of the complexities were included in the plan. They couldn't be, as there is no way to know what they would be. Instead of facing that fact head on, the business case including the implementation plan was signed off with enough 'contingency' to deal with the unexpected.

The system was finally launched late in 2010 for a total cost of over $25M AUD, more than 4 times over budget!

In addition to being $19M AUD over budget when it launched, the new Automated Payroll System required an additional 1,000 people to manually process the payroll, adding $1.15B AUD over 8 years and bringing the total cost to $1.2B AUD – more than 200 times over budget!

There are any number of reasons why the estimates were so spectacularly wrong. I'm sure there were earlier estimates higher than the original $6M AUD that leaders second-guessed and told the Project Managers were too high. I'm certain there were aspects of the process that were discovered by asking people what the process does instead of learning what it really does, and I'm confident that there was significant change to requirements after the project started. The "perfect plan" that took more than a year to create can never be perfect, but the biggest problem of all is that the plan cannot include the things we will learn along the way.

The closer you are to finishing the work, the more information you have. You learned more about what the customer wants each time you delivered something and received feedback. You learned more about the complexity of the work each time you faced a challenge and solved a problem. You learned more about your own capability each time a difficulty arose.

> THE FUTURE IS UNCERTAIN... BUT THIS UNCERTAINTY IS AT THE VERY HEART OF HUMAN CREATIVITY.
> Ilya Prigogine

That doesn't mean you have to wait until after you've finished to give an estimate. You still need to provide an idea of what you will have, when you will have it and how much it will cost or you won't get funding for anything.

What the Cone of Uncertainty provides is a way of understanding how to approach those estimates so you can still make meaningful commitments, but do so knowing the ambiguity and that you will learn the most important things after you start rather than trying to imagine them all before you begin. With that in mind and honesty at heart, you own up to uncertainty in the long term and ranges in the immediate term.

You're effectively saying:

> "With the information to hand, we expect that this large outcome will take between 6 months and 4 years. We could invest 12 months and millions of dollars in creating a plan that will be wrong, or we can start with something small that costs very little and delivers only a sliver of the value but will allow us to learn and refine our understanding. Which would you prefer?"

The Cone of Uncertainty also helps you to organise your work so you can meet those commitments.

Organising your work to meet the commitments while including the Cone of Uncertainty in your estimates means prioritising learning at the beginning of any large undertaking so you can invest in building relationships with those who will receive your output, so you can invest in understanding what they find valuable, and you can invest in understanding the true processes rather than the documented ones.

As you build your understanding through learning, you can start to transition to customer value by delivering functionality that creates valuable customer outcomes. The chances that it will be the right thing, work effectively without bugs and actually deliver value are hugely improved because of the learning you invested in.

Relative Estimation

Knowing that humans are terrible at estimating how long something will take, we need a different approach to estimation that doesn't rely on time.

Accepting that only those doing the work can make the commitments and they need to be included in the conversation about the problem to be solved as well as how we will go about solving it, we need a way to estimate that allows them to own the estimates and thereby own the commitments.

Acknowledging that we cannot foresee every difficulty that will arise or every complexity that will emerge, we need a way to estimate that incorporates the cone of uncertainty by allowing increasing flexibility the further out into the future a piece of work is.

The way to provide meaningful estimates that support real commitments is called relative estimation.

Rather than estimating using time and creating a fake sense of certainty that something complex will be completed by a certain date, relative Estimation uses the complexity or difficulty of a piece of work compared to similar work we have done before.

ESTIMATION

Instead of asking the people who will do the work how long the work will take, we ask them how difficult it will be relative to similar problems they have solved before.

When we're thinking about the difficulty of a piece of work, we explicitly separate ourselves from any consideration of how long it will take. Instead, we consider how complex it is, how uncertain it is, how much of it there is to do relative to the work we've done before.

A task that has many moving parts will be more complex than one that involves a single system, so our estimate should make it larger than similar work in a single system we've completed in the past.

Similarly, a task that involves something simple that we have done many times before but requires us to repeat it 100 times will be estimated as larger than a previously completed task that needed 10 repetitions.

Likewise, a task that we've never attempted before that includes a lot of uncertainty will have a larger estimation than a similar task we have previously completed that was somewhat understood when commencing it.

Separating our thinking from time-based estimation to size-based relative estimation is not an easy thing for an agile individual or team to adapt to. It

> A KEY TENET OF AGILE ESTIMATING AND PLANNING IS THAT WE ESTIMATE SIZE BUT DERIVE DURATION.
> Mike Cohn

takes practice and dedication, and we need to stick with it if we want to get better at it.

Just because it's difficult doesn't make it an invitation to chicken out of doing it! I've seen many teams go about an activity they call relative estimation where they estimate size using a numbered points system, but they have defined a period of time for each of the estimate values. So, for example, 1 point equals 1 day, 2 points equals 2 days, 5 points equals a week, etc. If you're using a time translation to points system, you're kidding yourself and your thinking is still based on how long it will take rather than relative size. You're not getting any of the benefits of relative estimation, so stop it right now.

Estimating size without thinking about time is difficult, as already mentioned. You can make it easier to do if you apply a sizing mechanism that is completely removed from time. In a lot of agile software teams, they use a scale called story points, but we're looking for a method that doesn't apply just to software and is also easy to apply as an individual. Another common technique that is easy to apply to any sort of work is t-shirt size.

ESTIMATION

When you first try relative estimation, it is helpful to establish a baseline of work you have recently completed that you can relate each new work item to. Whether as an individual or as a team, you'll need something to compare a piece of work to if you want to give it a size-based estimate.

Looking back on the work items you have finished, identify an item that represents the smallest thing you would normally do. Call that an extra small. Next, look for the largest item you would regularly take on and call that an extra-large.

If your extra-large item takes weeks to complete, then it's wise to think of those past items as simply too big. As discussed in the section on Backlogs, you want to break work down into individual work items of a few days at most. If that isn't possible, then at least strive to get them smaller than a week. The largest thing you arrive at becomes your baseline for the extra-large size. Remember, you are measuring against a task, not an entire project or deliverable!

Some people find it helpful to also set a baseline for the medium task as an item that is around halfway between the size of the extra small and the extra-large items already identified. Remember that by 'size,' we're not talking duration – so how long they take isn't the measure to use. Rather, measure them by how big they are considering their complexity, uncertainty and scale.

With the first few items selected, build up a broader understanding of the recently completed work by retrospectively estimating enough work items that you have a reasonable number of items of each size. This will help when it comes to using your baseline for estimating new work.

A simple technique to make this easier is to create 5 columns with the size headings and put each previously completed item into the column that best represents the size it had.

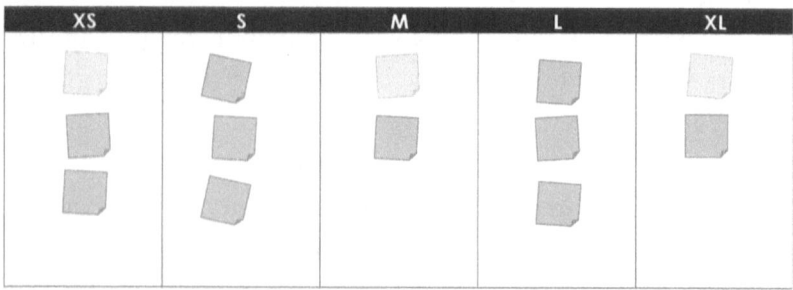

Now that you have your baseline in place, whenever estimating a new piece of work, you can very quickly and easily compare it to the baseline items.

When you have some clarity over what the task involves, you can ask yourself or your Team how big it is, compared to the baseline items. If this item it about the same size as your extra-small item, call it extra-small and move on. If it is somewhere between a medium and an extra-large, call it large.

That way, you can estimate very quickly, and you don't need to have documented every single detail, because you're not concerning yourself with how long it will take.

ESTIMATION

Honest forecasts and commitments

You now have a method of estimating that frees the people doing the work from having to consider how long something will take, and you've drastically reduced the cost of estimating itself, but you still need to make forecasts and commitments. These need to be meaningful, honest and achievable and they need to answer the question, "when will we have it?"

> *BEING HONEST MAY NOT GET YOU A LOT OF FRIENDS, BUT IT'LL ALWAYS GET YOU THE RIGHT ONES.*
> *John Lennon*

So how do you make those commitments when the people doing the work are not indicating in any way how long something will take, just how big it is?

The answer is that when forecasting and committing to deliverables in agile ways of working, we estimate using size and then derive time from that.

You've already classified a bunch of previously-completed work into size groupings and you have the benefit of 20:20 vision in hindsight because you already know how long each item took.

Add the time it took to complete each of the items you used to create your baseline, then look across each group and define the range of times for each size. You'll end up with something that you can use to derive duration.

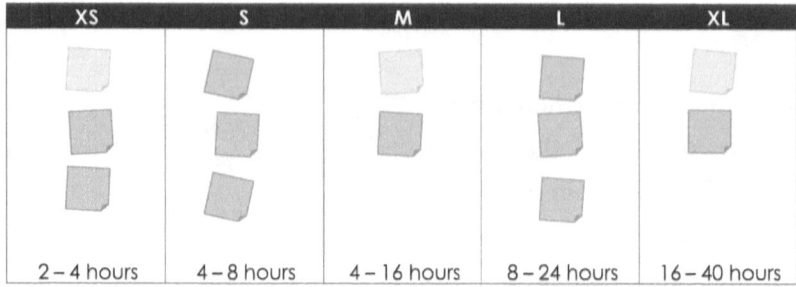

Now whenever an estimate is given, you can derive the duration and add it up for all the items in the backlog. Make sure you only refer to these time derivations AFTER estimating relative size and don't fall into the trap of including them in the conversation up front.

Rather than estimating an absolute time with the need to build in enough contingency to cater for everything that might go wrong, knowing that you'll often miss things, you can now give a range and be confident that the majority of your work will fall between that range.

When asked "when will we have it?", you can confidently and honestly give a forecast. "Based on our recent performance and the work we've identified, we'll be finished sometime between X and Y."

A word of caution though: people don't naturally switch to size-based estimates at the flick of a switch. When you create your baseline, it will be incredibly difficult to avoid thinking about how long a previously-completed item took when considering its size relative to other work. It is difficult to avoid that when you're baselining your own work, and it is even more difficult when completing this as a team.

Accept that this practice won't be perfect, but it will be valuable – it helps when having the conversation with those involved. At first it will seem counter-intuitive and unnatural, but stick with it and you will get better at it over time. As you improve, the overlap between the different sizes will diminish and your estimates will become more and more precise.

Activity

Check your estimates.

Have a look at your to-do list for the coming week or so.

Other than meetings or activities that are naturally timeboxed, write down the things you are looking to achieve. Give each one a familiarity rating out of 10 for how familiar you are with that task, where 1 means it is an entirely new task that you have never attempted before, and 10 means you are a master at it and have done it many times before.

When you start each one, write down the start date and time. As you complete each one, write down the end date and time and calculate the difference between the start and end time.

Task	Familiarity rating	Start date and time	End date and time	Total duration

What emerged from this activity?

Was there a variation between how long you estimated an activity to take and how long it actually took?

Was there a relationship between how familiar the work was and how accurate your estimate was?

CHAPTER 4

PRIORITISATION

An agile individual ensures they are always working on the most valuable things.

Working on the most valuable things means being able to assess the value of things and rank all of those things against each other.

It is not easy to understand the value of things. Valuation requires constant attention so you can keep your priorities up to date, and when the time comes to pick the next task to work on you can be confident that it is the most valuable one.

Being able to prioritise work based on what is most valuable means you first need to agree what valuable means to you.

> *THE KEY IS NOT TO PRIORITISE WHAT'S ON YOUR SCHEDULE, BUT TO SCHEDULE YOUR PRIORITIES.*
> Stephen Covey

If it is customer value, then you might need to talk to some real customers to find out what they value. If it is business value, then you'll need to understand what your business values (it might not be as simple as profit.)

In addition to a good understanding of the value of a piece of work, you also need to understand the cost. This could be expressed as dollars, effort, time or complexity. However you decide to assess the cost, each item will need to be assessed before you can prioritise.

Very often there will be 2 sides to the equation: one side that represents the value and the other that represents the cost. It's very much like determining the return on investment.

In traditional projects, the entire thing is defined before you begin and what needs to be done is defined as 'scope', which is presented on a timeline based on when resources are available with tight dependencies between each task with the overall project optimised for efficiency.

Thinking of all the work up front as scope, and sequencing it as if we can pre-empt everything that might go wrong, means we are working on things in order of scope. We finish absolutely everything about laying down the infrastructure before we start on building the system. We tried to plan for everything up front, so we invest more than we need to in infrastructure than we need to get started on the system, because that is more efficient than engaging the infrastructure people several times throughout the project.

PRIORITISATION

Approaching work in this way means we can only achieve a return on investment after everything is completely completed.

Inevitably, things go wrong somewhere. I've never heard of a project that didn't have some difficulties along the way. These difficulties make one or more of the tasks that we planned take longer than expected, or we find that the finances of the project get consumed faster than we expected, or we find that there are changes in the requirements because we didn't know about some of the questions we needed to ask.

When the time runs out or the finances dry up, we've delivered a lot of what needed to be done, but in the order of efficient work not in order of value – so some of the most valuable stuff doesn't get done and some of the least valuable stuff got done so far beyond where it needs to be, it was 'gold plated.'

To avoid investing too much in low-value activities and the potential of missing out all together on high-value activities, an agile individual prioritises their work based on cost and value.

But how do you determine cost and value?

The bad news is, it isn't simple or easy to come up with either cost or value and it is especially difficult when you're starting out on something new.

The temptation is to invest a great deal of effort and analysis in attaching numbers to each piece of work that needs to be completed, but no matter how much analysis you do, you'll be wrong more often than you're right. When you're starting out on a new endeavour, you haven't had the opportunity to put anything in the hands of your customer yet, so you haven't had any feedback or learning about what they really value.

You can certainly apply some design thinking or other tools to help you understand your customer's needs and desires better, but you are still starting from a low base of knowledge and most of what you decide in terms of cost and value will be guesswork.

The good news is that you don't need to know absolute numbers at the beginning. Guessing is OK at this point. The important outcome of applying a cost and value number to each of the pieces of work you're about to do is that you start with the most valuable things.

Starting with the most valuable things means you just need to know the cost and value of each item relative to the other items.

The first thing to do is to list out all the things that need to be done and break them down into small pieces of work.

Let's work up an example of the teenager who needs to clean their room.

When you have broken down the whole of what needs to be done into small pieces (such as "make the bed" or "pick up dirty

PRIORITISATION

All the stuff I need to do

clothes"), you can simply start with one item and compare it to another.

Is this item more valuable or less valuable than this other item?

Lay them out in a single horizontal row in order of value with the lowest value items on the left and the highest value items to the right.

In this example, we started with, "Make the bed," and then compared the relative importance of that with, "Sweep the floor." They decided that making the bed is more important than sweeping the floor, so they positioned it to the right.

It might seem counter intuitive to put the more valuable items to the right, as we'd normally list the most important things first, but this is only one step in building up a prioritisation model, it will make more sense once the model is complete.

BE AGILE

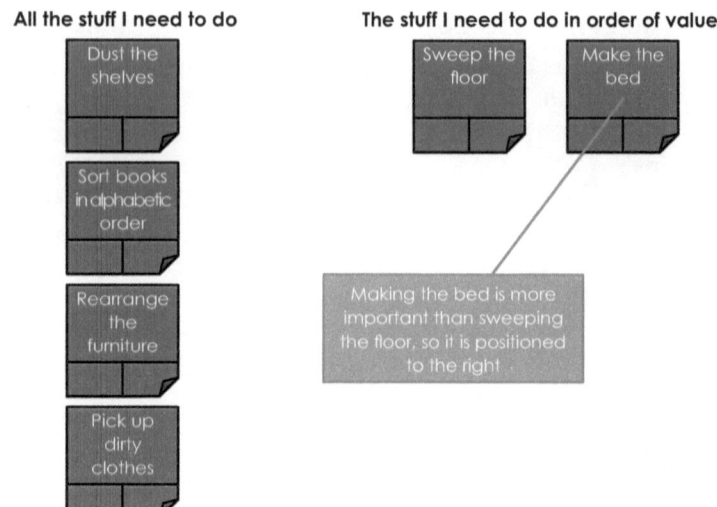

You then take the next item and compare its importance with the 2 items already assessed. In our example, it would be, "Dust the shelves."

Is dusting the shelves more valuable than making the bed? If no, it goes to the left and we compare it to the next item already in the list. If yes, we position it to the right. In this case, we decided that dusting the shelves is less valuable than both.

PRIORITISATION

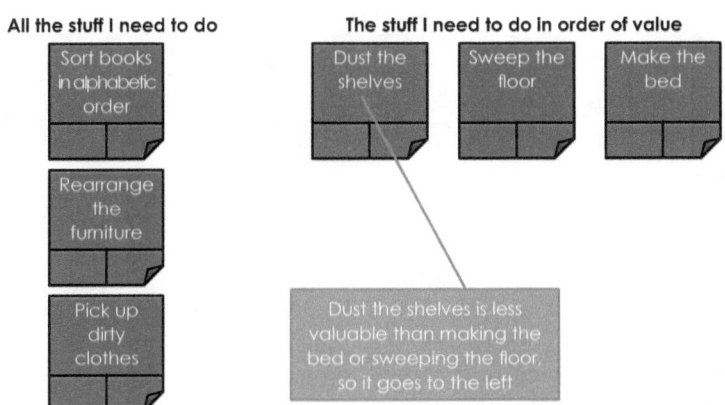

We continue with each item in the list, comparing it to all the items already assessed one at a time to decide where in the horizontal row it belongs.

Make sure you choose one thing over another each time. It is tempting to allow items to have the same value and group them together, but you cannot do two things at the same time. Multi-tasking doesn't work, so you'll have to choose one over another.

You'll also need to apply common sense: some things just have to be done before others, regardless of how much the customer values them. In our example, you wouldn't be able to sweep the floor without first picking up the clothes, so picking up the clothes cannot be placed at a lower importance than sweeping the floor.

When you've assessed all the items against each other, you'll end up with a single horizontal row of all your items in order of importance from left (least important) to right (most important).

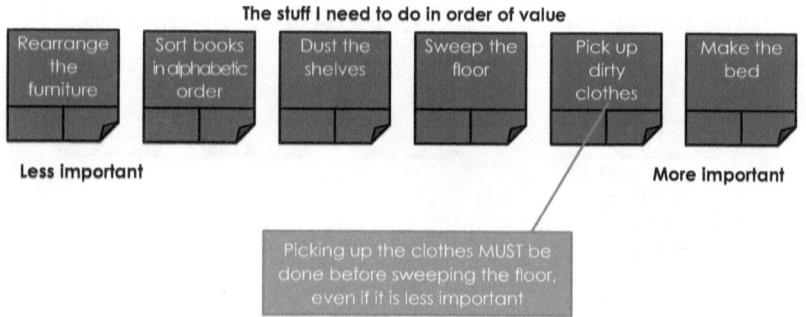

We now have a picture of how important each item is in relation to all the other items. It doesn't matter that we don't have absolute numbers to represent that value. We know that making the bed is more important than rearranging the furniture. The order of importance is the value side of the equation.

Before we launch into doing the work, we also need to assess our items based on their relative cost.

We could perform a lot of analysis to understand how long each item would take, but that would require us to know a lot more about what they are and the pace at which our teenager can work.

As with the value, we can use a relative assessment. How long each item takes doesn't matter as much as having an understanding of which ones take longer than the others.

Where we used a horizontal axis for the value, we'll use a vertical axis for the cost or effort, again assessing each item against the others with the lower cost items positioned higher so we have a natural order of working on things going from top to bottom. Working in order of value, the first item we assess is making the bed. We simply drop it down below the others as the starting point maintaining its horizontal position.

Next we consider picking up the clothes: will that take more or less effort than making the bed? We decide that picking up the clothes takes less effort than making the bed so it is positioned vertically higher.

Once we finish this we'll effectively have a diagonal alignment with the most important and easiest things at the top right and the least important things that are also the hardest at the bottom left.

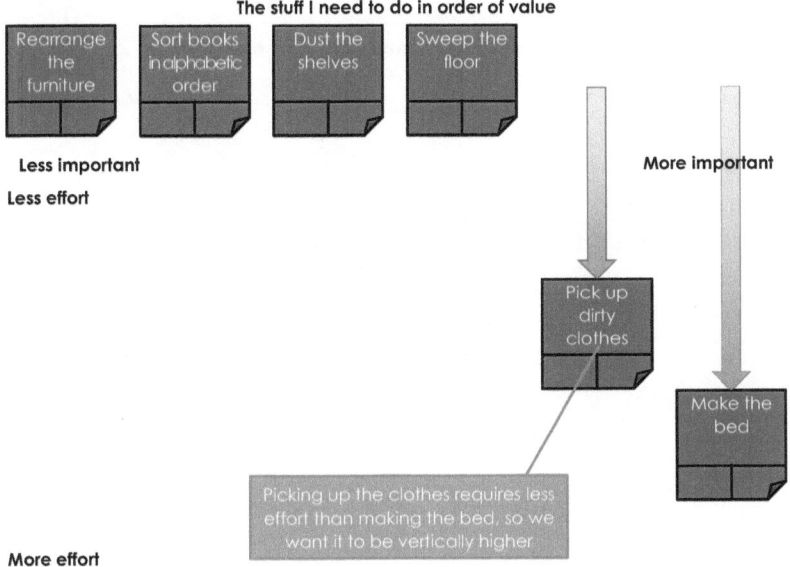

We continue with each of the remaining items, remembering to apply the common sense approach. For example, picking up the clothes MUST be done before we can sweep the floor, so regardless of how much effort they are relative to each other, picking up the clothes has to be positioned vertically higher.

Each item gets assessed against each of the other items that are already positioned. We don't just blindly put them in a position based on their relative effort though, the end result of this activity is a clear priority of what needs to be done first, so if an item simply must be done before another item, then it has to be positioned higher up.

For each relative assessment, we simply ask ourselves, "Is this item easier to do than this other item?"

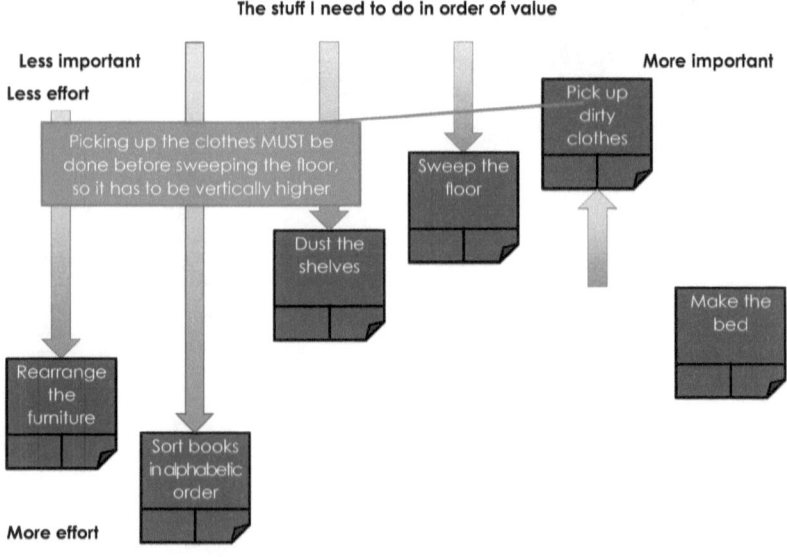

PRIORITISATION

We can then apply numbers to simplify our overall assessment. Number each item for its relative effort and importance so that the most important and the easiest items get the highest number.

This can be counter-intuitive because we are used to estimating how difficult things are rather than how easy they are.

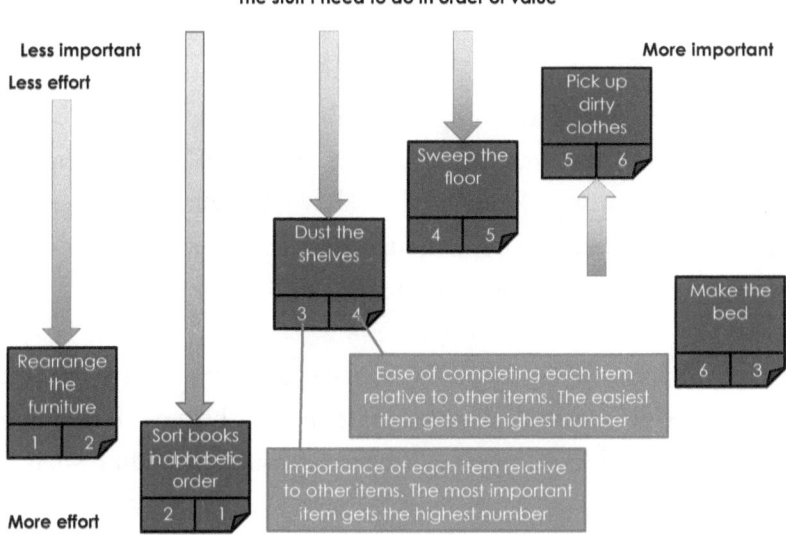

Using the numbering approach, we can then create a simple overall priority score for each item by multiplying its relative importance by its relative ease and then order our list of tasks based on the resulting priority number.

Task	Importance	Ease	Priority
Pick up the dirty clothes	5	6	30
Sweep the floor	4	5	20
Make the bed	6	3	18
Dust the shelves	3	4	12
Sort the books in alphabetic order	1	2	2
Rearrange the furniture	2	1	2

You'll notice that rearranging the furniture and sorting the books ended up with the same priority score. That's OK; it will happen often enough. Just pick one to place above the other. In this example, we've decided that even though they ended up with the same score, we want to sort the books first.

Another approach you might like to try is to place a matrix across it to help decide how to deal with each item. This helps with deciding how to approach it as much as it helps with understanding what is more important.

PRIORITISATION

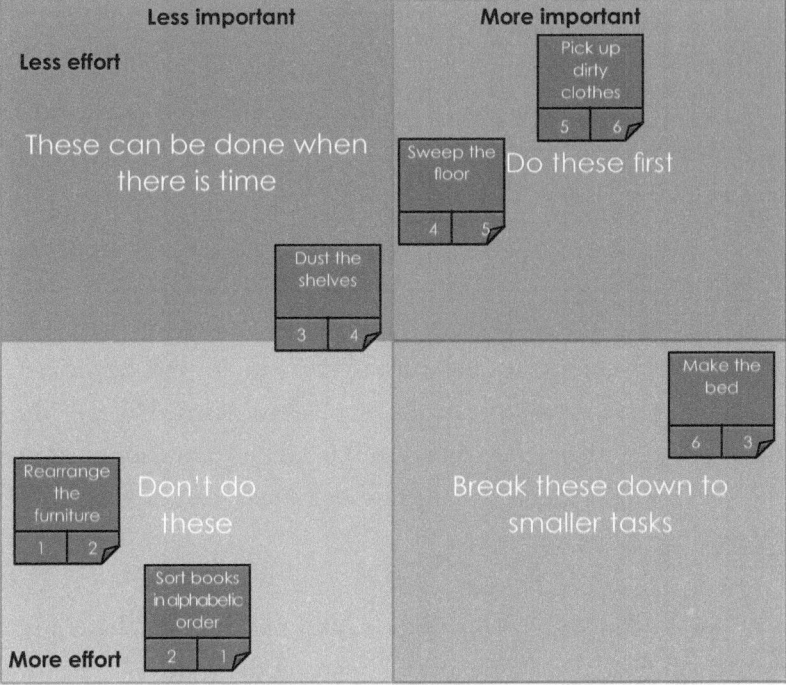

Using the importance and effort axes to create another visualisation of our priorities so we can think about then differently helps to know what to do for each item.

Items in the top right quadrant are important and they don't take too much effort, so we should get on with them first.

Items in the bottom right quadrant are important, but they will take more effort than our other items, so we should break them down into smaller tasks before attempting to complete them. Quite likely some of the smaller tasks we break them down into will not be as valuable as the overall.

Items in the top left quadrant are not as important as our other tasks, but they are easy to complete. These can be done when we have a small slice of time available.

Items in the bottom left are not especially valuable AND they take a lot of effort, so don't do them at all. It can be immensely difficult to say no to these things, but the truth of the matter is that by the time you get to these items in your list, you'll have learned about other things the customer values more, so it would be more honest to say they will not be done so you establish a more honest expectation of what will be delivered.

If you do get through everything else and the items you had in the bottom left quadrant are the most important things to do next, they will re-emerge, but keeping them in your backlog means you will waste time and effort looking at them every time you review your backlog.

Activity

Prioritise your work.

Put together a list of the things you need to do towards something you're looking to achieve. Rank them according to their relative importance and effort.

PRIORITISATION

The stuff I need to do in order of value

	Less important	More important
Less effort	These can be done when there is time	Do these first
More effort	Don't do these	Break these down to smaller tasks

Score them by the position they end up in and calculate their priority.

BE AGILE

Task	Value	Cost	Priority

CHAPTER 5

EXPERIMENTATION

Everything can be an experiment.

When coaching teams on how they might take an experimental mindset to their work, I most often hear that we can't take the risk of running experiments and that we just have to do what we've been asked to do.

Those same teams may be struggling to deliver value due to changes in requirements, unexpected complexities or any number of reasons. They've managed to convince themselves that there is certainty in what they're attempting to do even after repeated difficulties due to things that could not be known in advance.

Teams facing these struggles will often hunker down and invest more and more effort in attempting to generate that certainty before starting something. But... we cannot know everything in advance.

The more we try to understand all the unknowns up front and convince ourselves that the task at hand is simple, the more we are kidding ourselves that we can control complexity through analysis and the less likely we are to succeed.

A mindset for experimentation is really just a way of approaching work that acknowledges that we don't know everything, and we cannot eliminate the unexpected things that will emerge after we get started. An experimentation mindset recognises that we cannot know everything up front and that we need to learn as we go and apply that learning to what we do. Too much effort analysing everything we want to do will be completely wasted as it cannot include the things we will learn along the way.

One of the great things about using experiments to define your work is that it involves a lot of the analysis you are probably already doing.

You need to know the current state of your product or process, a warts-and-all assessment of the things about it that bring delight or cause difficulty for the people who use it, support it, consume it or otherwise interact with it. The current state should be as honest and complete as it can be and should involve input from anyone who is impacted by it or who wants to impact it.

You also need to have a desired state clearly defined. This is not to suggest that the desired state is a fake clarity of what the product or process will have. Steer clear of anything resembling features or functions. Instead, define your desired state by the outcomes it creates for the people who interact with it.

EXPERIMENTATION

When you achieve some clarity over your desired state, you need to define how you will measure that you have achieved it. This is the "one metric that matters."

The one metric that matters not only helps you to measure whether or not you are achieving the desired outcomes, it also offers ideas for how you will go about it and helps you to know when to stop. This metric needs to be a real, measurable metric that genuinely indicates that you are getting closer to your desired state.

Do not fall into the trap of using false or vanity metrics simply because they are easier to track. For example, let us imagine you provide services that your customers access online, but there are elements of your service that people cannot achieve online and they need to phone your contact centre. Your desired state might be that people can self-serve one of those elements. Measuring the cost of providing that specific element of your service may be a measurable metric that matters. Measuring the number of people that complete the self-service form on the other hand, while probably easier to measure, may mask the fact that people did not achieve what they wanted and are still needing to call the contact centre and you didn't actually achieve the outcome.

If the one metric that matters is not currently monitored or is difficult to baseline, you might need to build something that makes it possible to measure. Do not let that be an excuse to use an easier to track metric. In the example above, you may not know the cost of that particular call centre service or you might know the cost of the call, but not the cost of any processing that happens after the call.

Do your best to select a quantitative metric rather than a qualitative one. Sometimes this is not possible or requires so much effort that it will bog you down in preparation for too long. Where possible and the effort is not too significant, a quantitative metric will be much more valuable in assessing success.

Whatever metric you choose, it should measure what matters: the outcome to people.

The next thing to consider is a control metric. The control metric needs to be just as real, measurable and meaningful as the one metric that matters, but rather than tracking whether you are achieving your outcome, it measures an underlying product or process element that you want to ensure is not damaged through your changes towards the desired state.

In the example we used above, where we want to help people achieve something through self-service that they previously had to make a phone call for, you might choose repeat sales as a control metric. It might be that people who phone your call centre are more likely to order another product and we wouldn't want sales to go down because we reduced the cost of customer service.

With an honest understanding of the current state, a good idea of where you're going with the desired state and how you will measure it, you should look at the risks and assumptions that are implicitly included in the desired state's definition by asking some exploratory questions.

- Who wants the desired state (or would want it if they knew about it)?
- Why do they want it?
- How do we know they would want it?
- How would we know that it is delivering the desired benefit? This should be expressed as something measurable, the most direct metric that proves beyond doubt that we have achieved the desired outcome. We will call this the, "One metric that matters."
- How would we know we haven't broken something else? This should also be expressed as something measurable, the most direct metric that shows that in our efforts to create something new we haven't damaged the most important reason our product or process exists. We will call this the "control metric."
- What benefit will they receive?
- How have they lived without it for so long?
- What are they doing today to overcome not having it?
- Why don't we have it already?

The next step is to break down the desired state into small simple steps we could take on the journey towards it. Each one will become a target state that gets us closer to the desired state. We don't need to define every single target state that will deliver the full desired state. It might take us years to realise the full desired state and we'll learn a great deal along the way that will change what we target and how we go about it. The focus should be on targets that are nearby. Understanding the smallest simplest things we can do that gets us closer, and is more valuable than understanding everything we need to do to get all the way there.

With a few target states defined, we can prioritise them relative to each other, ensuring that the first few target states are in some logically sensible priority order if they depend on each other.

When we have the smallest simplest thing that gets us closer to the desired state, we call this the "next target state." This will form the basis for our first experiment.

Using the same example as earlier, our next target state might be a simple form on your website accessible through the customer's "My Account" page with entirely manual back-end processing and responses.

At this point, you can start filling out an experiment iterations canvas.

To start with, just fill in the top sections: Date, Product, Desired State and Owner along with the one metric that matters, the control metric and their current values.

You can download an editable template at https://www.terryhaayema.com/templates

EXPERIMENTATION

Experiment Iterations Canvas

Date:
Product:
Desired State:
Owner:

	The once metric that matters	Control metric
	The metric that shows we are getting closer to the desired state	The metric that shows we haven't broken something important
	Current Value	Current Value

	1	2	3	4	5	6
Outcome						
Hypothesis						
Method						
Criteria						
	Execute the Experiment					
Result						
Learning						

Derived from the Bloom Lean Experiment Canvas Released under Creative Commons 4.0 licence which is itself inspired by the Javelin Experiment Board

The experiment iterations canvas is a handy tool where you can capture your thinking about the experiments you want to run that will get you closer to your desired state.

Don't invest too much time in the experiments that are off in the future. Capture the outcomes you defined as each target state, but wait until you get to each one to define the hypothesis, method and criteria. That way you will always include your latest learning when you define each experiment.

Considering the next target state, we repeat the assessment of the risks and assumptions that we performed for the desired state, but at the now smaller and more immediate scale.

The risks we are assessing are things that impact us if they occur while the assumptions are things that impact us if they do not occur.

We are looking for the riskiest risk, or the most impactful assumption. With an understanding of our riskiest risk or assumption we can get to work on formulating a hypothesis.

One of the most significant benefits of approaching work as an experiment is that it forces us to formulate a hypothesis. Using a hypothesis to define what needs to be done avoids creating the perception that we have any certainty over the solution. Instead, it provides real clarity of what needs to happen and how we will know if it is any good.

EXPERIMENTATION

With everything we have done towards our experiment so far, we can create a hypothesis using a simple format which we may reword later if it turns out to be more elegant to do so.

We believe that ...<solution>... will ...<outcome>... within ...<time period>... ,
We will know this is true when ...<metric>... .

Using the same example as earlier, you might arrive at a hypothesis like this:

We believe that allowing people to manage their own address details will reduce calls to the contact centre within 1 month.
We will know this is true when address change request calls to the contact centre reduce by 10%.

You will note that the metric for our first experiment is different to the one we defined as the one-metric-that-matters. This is fine, and not unusual. Each experiment needs to have a way to measure whether or not that particular hypothesis is proven, disproven or inconclusive. Some experiments will utilise the one-metric-that-matters as their success criteria, and some will not.

Check your hypothesis for any bias. Are you emotionally invested in proving something? Your hypothesis may slant your approach if it aligns to your current beliefs. Often a simple change in the wording will help to create a hypothesis that helps reduce bias and informs a more empirical approach.

Ensure your hypothesis provides a learning opportunity. You don't want to run your experiment simply to prove what you are already thinking, but rather to learn something. An experiment where you want to prove something will often be flawed and lead to nothing more valuable than a fake sense of being right. An experiment that is free of any up-front desires will be more likely to prove or disprove something and will also provide far greater opportunities to learn something new about the space you are in.

Now it is time to poke your head up and have a look around. Are there any other things going on in the domain you are hoping to experiment in that might muddy the waters and make it difficult to know whether your experiment made an impact?

In our example above, the contact centre management may be planning to reroute address change requests to different operators or split them by the state the caller is in, making your job of baselining and collecting metrics more difficult. Maybe they are planning to ask outbound sales calls to confirm the addresses of everyone they speak to, reducing the number of calls, or maybe they're planning to send out an email letting customers know that we will be better able to serve them if their address details are up to date and thereby increasing the number of calls.

Look externally too: there may be things happening in the external environment that will impact the metric you want to use to measure your experiment.

EXPERIMENTATION

If you find that there are complicating events or activities that will impact the same measures you want to use, then you may need to do one of the following:

- Define a different metric
- Delay your experiment until after the complicating events are finished
- Arrange for the complicating events to be delayed until after your experiment is completed
- Find a way to filter the impacts of the complicating events
- In the worst case, you may need to completely redefine your experiment

You now have a clear idea of the riskiest risk or assumption in your area, a clearly defined and testable hypothesis, a step-by-step method and some confidence that the metrics used won't be impacted by other unrelated complicating events. It is now time to get that all onto an experiment canvas.

Experiment Canvas

Experiment Definition

Riskiest Assumption or Risk

Testable Hypothesis

We believe that: _____

Will drive: _____

Within: _____

We will know this
is true when: _____

Method

Experiment Results

Results

Conclusion
☐ Proven
☐ Disproven
☐ Inconclusive

Learnings and next steps

Derived from the Experiment Canvas released by Design A Better Business under Creative Commons 4.0 Licence

EXPERIMENTATION

The left side of the experiment canvas is where we capture the details of the experiment we want to run. If we're using an experimentation approach for our day-to-day work, then it gives us the chance to think about it differently. We're now adding success criteria in the form of a measurable metric as well as clearly defining the method we will use.

Use the "Riskiest assumption or risk" box to capture the most impactful risk or assumption from the analysis earlier.

In the "Testable hypothesis" box, formulate the hypothesis described earlier, confirming that the metric ("We will know this is true when,") is a real success measure and not a vanity metric or merely the easiest one to baseline and track.

Plan out the steps you will take in executing the experiment in the "Method" box being careful to define a method that supports an effective experiment.

- Include any setup or clean up steps.
  Do you need to baseline the metric first, or do you already have it?
  How will you collect the metric once the, "Within," period has elapsed?
  Are there any elements of your experiment that need to be cleaned up afterwards?
- Is it possible to define a control group?

If possible, it will help to understand if your experiment is proven, disproven or inconclusive by leaving a subset of the total unchanged so you can demonstrate the impact of the changes
- How much can you reduce the "observer effect"
When making the changes as an experiment, you become the observer. The mere fact that the changes are being observed will impact the result. Try to eliminate yourself and your observations as much as possible from the actions or changes taking place. If you can step back entirely and simply measure the results after the, "Within," period, you will go a long way towards achieving this.

Execute the experiment as per the method.

Gather the results. Try to be as objective as possible when gathering the results and be sure to record as much information as possible about the outcome of the experiment.

- What happened?
- What did you observe?
- What aspects of the implementation as well as the outcome were unexpected?
- Were there any other things going on that might have impacted the metric or the influence and impact of your experiment?

Reflect on the overall outcome.

EXPERIMENTATION

Activity

Define and execute an experiment.

Think about something complex you might be working on.

If it is described as work, how could you rewrite the description as an experiment so you can define the learning opportunity contained within it?

First define the outcome that would form the "North Star" of these experiments.

How would you measure progress towards your North Star? This becomes your "One metric that matters."

What should you measure to ensure you haven't broken anything important? This is your "Control Matric."

Add these to the metrics section of the Experiment Iterations Canvas.

Now, break down the North Star outcome into smaller outcomes you can test along the way.

Fill in an experiment canvas for the first experiment. Remember to use the basic hypothesis format until you have practiced enough to create your own.

BE AGILE

*We believe that ...<solution>... will ...<outcome>...
within ...<time period>... ,
we will know this is true when ...<metric>... .*

With the experiment canvas complete, go back to the experiment iterations canvas and fill in the hypothesis, method, and criteria you will test against.

Now complete the experiment.

***

Even if you don't actually complete the experiment, thinking through your work as if it is an experiment allows you to get explicit in how you will test your hypothesis and what you will learn as an outcome. Both are valuable in and of themselves.

Of course, completing the experiment is even more valuable, so please do give experimentation a genuine try before you dismiss it as too hard.

EXPERIMENTATION

Experiment Iterations Canvas

Date:	Product:
Desired State:	Owner:

	The one metric that matters	Control metric
	The metric that shows we are getting closer to the desired state	The metric that shows we haven't broken something important
	Current Value	Current Value

	1	2	3	4	5	6
Outcome						
Hypothesis						
Method						
Criteria						
	Execute the Experiment					
Result						
Learning						

Experiment Canvas

Experiment Definition	Experiment Results
Riskiest Assumption or Risk	**Results**
Testable Hypothesis We believe that: _____ Will drive: _____ Within: _____ We will know this is true when: _____	**Conclusion** ☐ Proven ☐ Disproven ☐ Inconclusive **Learnings and next steps**
Method	

CHAPTER 6

Make Work Visible

An agile individual makes their work visible so they can manage it better.

Making work visible is more than just having a to do list.

When work is visible, everyone involved can instantly see what is happening, the progress of a task, what has been done and the work that is coming up.

There are various techniques you can use to make work visible; the best-known approach is the Kanban board.

The Kanban board is one element of the Kanban manufacturing system developed at Toyota by Taiichi Ohno in the 1940s to improve efficiency. We won't go too deep into Kanban itself, but let's take a look at the Kanban board to see how it can help you to make work visible.

A Kanban board presents the flow of work through the workflow of an endeavour with each step in the workflow represented as a column containing the work items currently in that step. In the biscuit baking example, it would have:

- Gather ingredients
- Mix ingredients
- Rolling and cutting
- Baking
- Packaging
- Delivering

Each work item is represented as a card that flows through the process so at any time we have visibility of the supply and demand for each step in our process. In the manufacturing process, the card would travel with the materials or product so we can always see how much we have, how much we've used and how much we need to replenish.

For personal productivity, we'll leave the cards on the board as they travel through the system of work.

Once the workflow is known, you can create a board to make it visible.

Gathering	Mixing	Rolling & cutting	Baking	Packaging	Delivering

With the Kanban board in place, you can add the cards to show where each item is at in the process. Post-It® Notes make ideal cards as they are easy to move between workflow steps.

Gathering	Mixing	Rolling & cutting	Baking	Packaging	Delivering
Choc-Chip #1245		Ginger Nut #1244		Short Bread #1242	Choc-Chip #1241
		Vanilla Biscuits #1243			Anzac Biscuits #1240

We can now see what each step in the process is working on by looking at the cards in that step's column. The cards in each column represent the inventory held at that step.

We can also see that mixing and baking are currently idle and that rolling and cutting has 2 things in progress, so we may have a bottleneck in our process.

We need to understand the capacity of each step in the process if we want to know when a step is overloaded and holding additional inventory. Any step that has too much inventory is creating waste and slowing down the end-to-end process.

The capacity for each step in a Kanban system is managed through limiting Work In Progress, or WIP Limits. Defining the capacity for each step helps us to know when it is approaching or exceeding its throughput limits. Let's add it to our Kanban board.

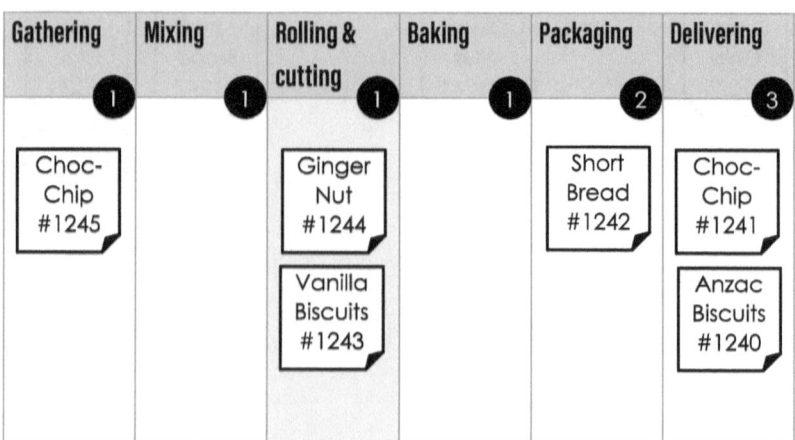

Now we can see that rolling and cutting has exceeded its capacity. Inventory will languish in that step creating waste and slowing down the end-to-end process.

Mixing, baking and packaging are operating at less than their capacity, which might be okay or it might not. Having identified that a step in our process is operating under capacity, we need to investigate why that is the case.

Our ability to exploit rolling and cutting will be enhanced by identifying at which point in the step the cards are sitting. Maybe they just arrived and are being worked on or maybe they are finished and waiting for the baking step to pick them up.

One method of doing this is to insert a column between each of our existing columns that shows when a step has completed its work and the card is waiting for the next step. In other words, we would insert a column between gathering and mixing called "Ready for mixing" and a column between mixing and rolling & cutting called "Ready for rolling & cutting," and so on.

Another approach is to represent the readiness for the next step by placing cards on the right side of the column. For this example, we'll use that approach, purely so we don't have to cram too many columns onto our board and make the labels too small to read.

Applying that to our board, we now have better visibility of what is happening in our system.

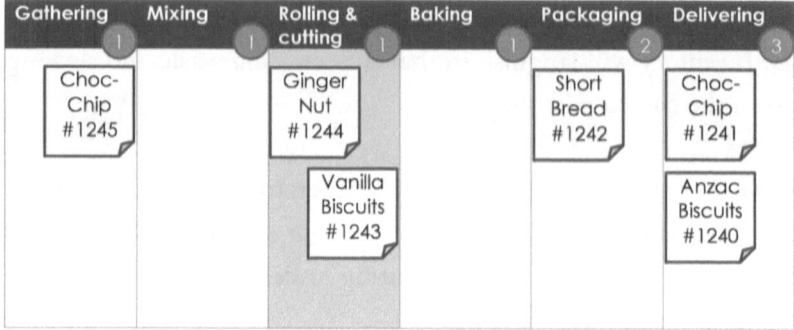

Now we can see that amongst the inventory held at rolling and cutting, the Vanilla Biscuits card is done and waiting for baking to pick it up. The original view that rolling and cutting has a problem has been enhanced so we can see that the problem might be with the baking step.

We can't know everything when we make work visible. It is worth noting that whatever problems or bottlenecks are exposed are indications of a problem, not pointers to a solution. It is often said that having visibility of the problem is an 'invitation to a conversation' and we need to have that conversation before we can understand the causes of the problem and consider what we might do to resolve it.

Wherever the problem lies and whatever solution we implement, we are better off having visibility of the issues so we can optimise the throughput of valuable customer outcomes and increase the efficiency of the overall system.

MAKE WORK VISIBLE

Activity

Create a Kanban board and use it to make work visible.

Thinking about the work that flows through your area, what is the flow of valuable customer outcomes? Identify the steps in your process.

You might use a large whiteboard or simply stick coloured tape on a wall to create your columns.

Label each column and add the capacity of each step in your process as the WIP Limit.

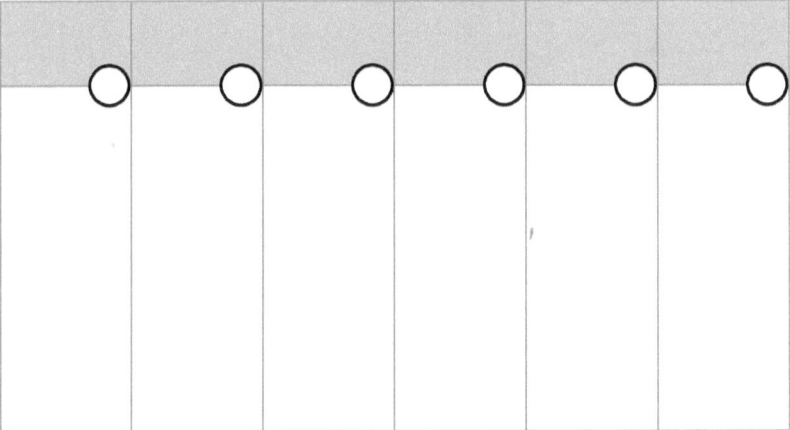

Then add the cards that represent the work currently in the system.

What insights can you draw from what you have made visible?

Insights from making work visible

CHAPTER 7

INCREMENTAL AND ITERATIVE

The agile individual works both incrementally and iteratively.

With the industrial age mindset, there is a belief that people who are smart enough can have sufficient knowledge about a context to be able to plan in advance everything that needs to happen to bring about a successful result.

When the smart people have defined the entirety of a thing and planned out every step, every action and every task in great detail, then it is up to the people who do the work to fulfill the plan.

The plans tend to be monumentally huge with the details for all the work defined up front. So much has been invested in creating the perfect plan, both financially and emotionally, that the originators of the plan become completely attached to it. Often, with so much work having gone into their plan, they need to prove it is a great plan and will go to enormous lengths to resist any form of change.

This emotional investment in being right and demonstrating that this is the perfect plan creates a mental pattern for 'prove.' We want to prove we are capable, that our work is valuable and that we know what we are doing. Any challenge to the plan can be a threat that might expose that we are not as capable as we want to be seen to be.

An agile mindset does not seek to create the perfect plan and then move to execute it. We know that there are aspects of the outcomes we want to bring about that cannot be fully known up front. We don't want to separate the people creating the plan from the people doing the work because we know that the people doing the work are much closer to the situation and often have more knowledge and capability when it comes to making decisions, so they are in the best position to do the planning.

> SMALL BATCHES OF WORK, SMALL TEAMS, SHORT CYCLES, AND QUICK FEEDBACK—IN EFFECT, "SMALL EVERYTHING."
> Stephen Denning, *The Age of Agile*

An agile mindset not only accepts that change is inevitable, it seeks out change in order for us to improve. For this reason, we keep the plan high level for the longer-term outcomes and explicitly add in points at which to reflect on how we're doing, what we can learn and adapt the plan accordingly.

Instead of needing to prove that the plan is the perfect one, we want to improve the plan as we go so that it always incorporates the latest

INCREMENTAL AND ITERATIVE

learning and adjusts to changes in our environment, our marketplace or ourselves.

This is where being iterative and incremental comes in.

When we approach something big iteratively, it means going over the same area time after time in short bursts with space in between each iteration where we consciously review what we have just done and adjust. These gaps in activity allow us to develop a mindset for 'improve.'

During each iteration, we add a small incremental improvement to what we already have, being careful to include how we will measure whether that increment has taken us closer to where we want to go in the longer term so that we have concrete information when we pause to improve and can be empirical in any decisions we take.

Each time we pause to learn, we review the plan and adapt based on the latest things we have learned. In that way, our plan continues to improve as we go. Rather than trying to create the perfect plan up front, we start with a high-level plan and refine it as we go along.

During the periods of work in each iteration, we focus on achieving something small and valuable, adding another increment into the overall solution. These short bursts of focused work allow us to invest all our skills, experience, and capability into something small enough to achieve quickly, usually a week or two. These periods of focus are the time when we want to 'prove' our ability to get the job done, to prove that we have the capability to deliver in the longer term by delivering a small chunk of it every week or two.

Every work period is a short burst of 'prove' and every pause for reflection, learning and replanning is a short burst of 'improve.'

Activity

Thinking about a large objective you're working towards, how could you make it more incremental and more iterative?

Maybe you're already working iteratively, delivering value in short bursts of activity that are divided by periods of reflection and improvement. If this is the case, then it might be most valuable to think about how you can become more incremental in what is delivered.

Are you completing the small things within each iteration? I couldn't tell you how many times I've coached people and teams who were working to a regular cadence of prove and improve but were still working on things that were too big to fit into the iteration.

Maybe you're already working incrementally, adding small discreet pieces to the longer-term objective with each one being completed before moving on to the next. If this is your situation, then maybe you'll get more value from thinking through how to get more iterative in the way you work.

Are you pausing regularly for reflection and improvement, at least every couple of weeks? How effective is your reflection at creating genuine improvement? I've seen many times people and teams that

INCREMENTAL AND ITERATIVE

pause for reflection regularly, but just have the same conversation over and over again, never defining anything they will actually take action on – and even if they do, they don't include a way to measure whether it is having the intended impact.

CHAPTER 8

Outcome Over Output

An agile individual focuses on the outcome of what they are working on and looks for ways to achieve that outcome with as little output as possible.

With industrial age thinking, an outcome is considered at the beginning of a major piece of work but very shortly after a solution that will deliver that outcome is defined, the outcome falls away from our attention as the details of the solution begin to capture our focus.

As our attention shifts to gathering the requirements of what needs to be delivered, the outcome drifts to the back of our minds and our ability to find creative ways to provide that outcome diminishes.

As requirements are gathered together, complexities emerge that mean we need to think about the impact of the solution on groups of people we haven't considered, and we need to collect information from areas we haven't investigated. We're going to find that we are depending on events happening elsewhere in the organisation and very soon, we've completely forgotten about the outcome and are consumed with delivering more and more output.

When we're happy we've got the requirements right, we start to work on delivering the solution. Here, we're getting caught up in the detail of the tasks being completed that will deliver the output, where the thinking is all about what we're doing not what we're achieving.

As we progressively get through the work, we're reporting on progress towards the output. Project status updates report on the status of a variety of factors in a project including risk, finances, scope, etc., they do report on the progress of delivery and whether we're 'on track' or falling behind schedule, but they don't report on progress towards the outcome.

I worked with a team several years ago that was working on a project to provide a document management capability. The outcome was to provide a way for people to be able to store and manage documents in a way that made them easier to find. Over time, the organisation had created an immense number of documents that were stored in a variety of systems that didn't connect to each other and people wasted enormous amounts of time trying to find things in the mess.

As the requirements were collected, each part of the organisation had a different way of thinking about their materials and everyone wanted something different in how they should be stored, searched for, retrieved, etc.

A great deal of output was generated, including reams and reams of documents about the planning, the requirements and specifications, the project and of course the system itself.

Within a very short period of delivering the solution, with a great deal of effort in cataloguing and organising documents from all across the organisation, people were organically storing their documents in the wrong places with ineffective file names and re-creating the mess they had had before.

Not only did the outcome fall away from our consciousness as we started working towards the output, but the result achieved no outcome whatsoever.

It might be hard to define what to do when you're obsessed about an outcome, but you remain creative in how you can deliver it.

If we had maintained our focus on the outcome, it would have become obvious at some point while gathering requirements that the variety of ways people were thinking about their documentation meant that a new system would not deliver what we were setting out to achieve.

Sometimes the outcome is lost before the question is even asked. People will come to you with a request for output with no thought in their mind about what the outcome is that triggered their request.

We see this all the time in technology teams. People have experienced a difficulty and immediately leap to the solution. This is only human; we are naturally problem solvers. Discussing it amongst themselves, they talk about the solution they have conceived, not the problem they're looking to solve.

When the need arrives with the technology team, it is already a solution. Instead of coming to the team with a problem to solve or an opportunity to exploit, it is an output. Rather than saying to the Team, "We have a problem where …," people will approach the Team with, "We need a button that …."

The Team, with all the best intentions, immediately leaps into how they might provide the button, rather than looking at what is the simplest and easiest way to provide the outcome.

If this is the case for you, regardless of the type of work you do, take a pause before considering how you might deliver the output. Ask some questions that can help you arrive at some clarity over what the outcome is.

- What problem will this solve?
- What outcome do we seek?
- Who is it a problem for?
- How many people experience this problem?
- Why don't we have that already?
- How will we know if we have achieved the outcome?

OUTCOME OVER OUTPUT

Activity

Redefine your outcomes.

Thinking about the work you're involved with now, are you working towards an outcome? Or is it an output?

Current work items	Is it an outcome?	What is the outcome?
	☐ Yes ☐ No	
	☐ Yes ☐ No	
	☐ Yes ☐ No	
	☐ Yes ☐ No	
	☐ Yes ☐ No	
	☐ Yes ☐ No	
	☐ Yes ☐ No	
	☐ Yes ☐ No	
	☐ Yes ☐ No	
	☐ Yes ☐ No	
	☐ Yes ☐ No	

BE AGILE

	☐ Yes ☐ No	
	☐ Yes ☐ No	
	☐ Yes ☐ No	
	☐ Yes ☐ No	
	☐ Yes ☐ No	
	☐ Yes ☐ No	
	☐ Yes ☐ No	

How can you provide those outcomes with less output?

CHAPTER 9

TIMEBOXING

An agile individual timeboxes their activities to generate the greatest value from the smallest time.

Timeboxing means setting a time period within which something will be done and then stopping when you get to the end of that period.

> PERFECT IS THE ENEMY OF GOOD.
> Voltaire

It might seem like you will abandon the value of what you're doing if you stop before you're finished, but that isn't the case.

Timeboxing is based on the "Pareto principle," (also known as the 80/20 rule,) which states that roughly 80% of effects come from 20% of causes.

When you establish a timebox for something, you focus the thinking on the highest priority aspects of it. Combined with ruthless prioritisation of work at all levels, timeboxing provides a way of driving quickly to outcomes rather than completing all the activities relating to outputs.

Imagine you are working towards an outcome, say for example making dinner for your family. The outcome is a happy, nourished family enjoying a meal together. Let's imagine you have decided to prepare a roast dinner with all the trimmings that will take 2.5 hours to prepare. In this case, the output is a roast dinner.

If you timebox the preparation of dinner to 30 minutes, you can still produce a delicious dinner, but you can't produce the roast and associated side dishes that you would have prepared if you gave it the full time. The output is diminished, but the outcome is achieved. You've literally provided 80% of the value with 20% of the activity.

Timeboxing also helps you to think differently when planning for a major piece of work. You might be defining the solution to a particular problem and thinking through all the things that need to be done to bring that solution into existence. Maybe it looks like it will take you around a year to complete this significant project, but what changes when you start asking, "What would we do if we only had a month to solve this problem?" Suddenly the output becomes too expensive or even impossible, but you still need to achieve the outcome.

"If we only had a month, the only thing we could do is … and that would only provide …."

Many times, when I've helped people think through the timeboxed approach, they have arrived at something that delivers the bulk of the outcome with a tiny portion of the time.

The timeboxing technique is especially valuable in meetings. Sometimes a conversation in a meeting goes on and on and no decision is reach and no real result is achieved. When you timebox a discussion, you focus the attention to those things that are most important to discuss.

Very often, more work is still required after the timebox is reached because the timeboxed activity left something more to be achieved, but the way it focused the thinking on the outcome and what was truly valuable was worthwhile in and of itself.

When you've reached the end of the timebox, you have a choice. Much of the outcome has been achieved, but there may remain something more to do. You can then have a conversation about extending the work to another timebox, possibly a smaller one.

If you do need to have another timebox, you can get specific about the outcome for the new timebox.

BE AGILE

Activity

Timebox a piece of work.

Select a piece of work you are about to embark on.

- What work is involved?
- What is the outcome?
- How long would you expect it would take?
- Give it a much shorter timebox.
- What can you do in the timebox that contributes to the outcome?

Work	Outcome	Usual time that work would take	Timebox	What can you do in the timebox?

When you have completed the work, return to this page and record your results.

TIMEBOXING

How did timeboxing change how I thought about the work?	What outcome was achieved?	What outcome remains?

CHAPTER 10

STOP STARTING AND START FINISHING

An agile individual limits the amount of work they have at any given time so that they can focus on the most important things.

Trying to do too many things at the same time leads to context switching, lower quality, frustration and means each thing takes longer to complete.

I've spoken to many people who believe that they are really good at multi-tasking and that having several things in progress is an effective way to work. The truth is very different: humans are not good at doing multiple things simultaneously and you will actually be dividing your attention into smaller, less effective portions.

Whenever you split your attention across more than one thing, you lose around 10% of your capacity either side of the split. This is because you need to release the thinking from one task when you pick up the threads of your thinking for the next task. You're effectively inserting wasteful effort in between each of the cognitive slices you're dividing all the work into.

That means that when you're doing one thing, you have 100% of your cognitive and creative abilities to bring to bear on that task, but when you're multi-tasking between 2 things, you only have 40% available for each one. The more things you're trying to work on at the same time, the less capacity you have for each one and the more effort is wasted in switching between the tiny slices.

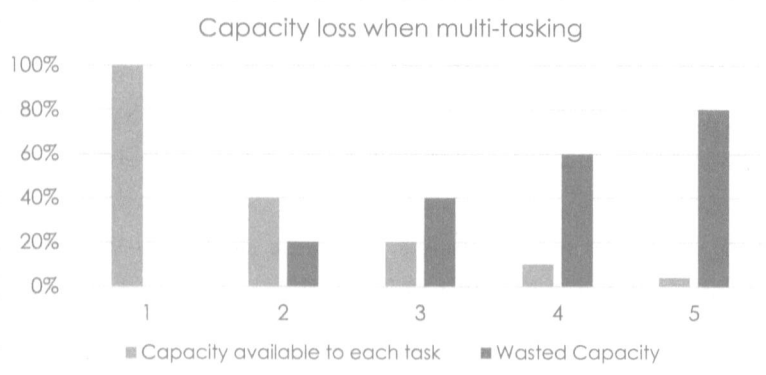

Number of simultaneous tasks	Capacity available to each task	Wasted capacity
1	100%	0%
2	40%	20%
3	20%	40%
4	10%	60%
5	4%	80%

STOP STARTING AND START FINISHING

Not only does multi-tasking reduce your overall effectiveness and create a lot of waste, it is also stressful and difficult. The reduced attention available for each task makes it a lot easier for mistakes to be made and reduces the overall quality of what you're doing.

Limiting how much work you have in progress allows you to focus with greater attention on the one thing you're doing at any given time.

In an ideal situation, you would start work on something and focus on it to the exclusion of everything else until it is finished.

> START A 'STOP DOING' LIST. I'LL LEAVE IT AS AN EXISTENTIAL DILEMMA ON WHETHER TO PUT THAT TASK ON YOUR TO DO LIST.
> James C. Collins

The real world isn't always ideal, though, and there are many circumstances where you will need to pause work on one thing and do something else.

When pausing something, be explicit with yourself: you are going to stop working on that item and start working on something else; if a development occurs on the first item that means you can get back to it, make sure you finish the second item before getting back to the first.

If you have a reason to expect that a piece of work may need to be paused before you start it, use that foresight to break the work into smaller pieces before you begin. Try to define the outcome of each piece and then work to achieve each outcome separately.

If for example, you are about to prepare a document that will need to be approved by your boss before it is socialised, break that work into 2 separate pieces. The first task is to prepare the document and submit it to your boss for approval. The second task is to share the document with the people who should receive it.

Let your boss know when you send them the document that you are now going to get on with the next item in your backlog of priorities, so it would be great if they can complete their review before the new task completes so you will be ready to get back to the document immediately after that task is completed.

Breaking the work into 2 smaller tasks allows you to have only one thing in progress and consider the work finished on each one individually. When the document goes for approval, you free up your attention to get on with the next thing you need to do. When your boss gets back to you with their approval, you will finish the task you're working on before picking up the second task of sharing the approved document.

You might think that this will reduce your efficiency, because the document might be your highest priority and surely it would be better to park the other work the moment your boss approves the document. Intuitively that feels correct, but it isn't.

You're an agile individual: you work iteratively and incrementally on small tasks that contribute to ongoing improvement, so the task you picked up when you submitted the document to your boss is not a mammoth task that will take weeks to complete. It will be done very soon so the document won't sit around for too long.

The focus on one thing at a time will increase the flow of your outcomes. The document might take slightly longer to get to the people it needs to be shared with, but you achieved three things in that time rather than one.

Working this way will allow you to invest a greater focus and attention into each thing you are doing. Having only one thing in progress means you will have far fewer things that are due or overdue, which reduces the amount of effort you need to keep following things up and reporting back to those who are waiting for them.

Having too many things on the go at once means you'll often be fielding queries from those who are waiting for something about when they will have it and why it is delayed. You'll spend a lot of your time 'putting out fires,' which is wasted effort that doesn't help deliver outcomes.

Focusing on one thing at a time enables fire prevention instead of firefighting.

Activity

Enable a focus on one thing at a time.

What do you currently have in progress?

Make a list and then decide which items can be split into what you will do now and what you will do later and which items can be stopped all together.

BE AGILE

Items in progress	Can it be split?	Can it be stopped?
	☐ Yes ☐ No	☐ Yes ☐ No
	☐ Yes ☐ No	☐ Yes ☐ No
	☐ Yes ☐ No	☐ Yes ☐ No
	☐ Yes ☐ No	☐ Yes ☐ No
	☐ Yes ☐ No	☐ Yes ☐ No
	☐ Yes ☐ No	☐ Yes ☐ No
	☐ Yes ☐ No	☐ Yes ☐ No
	☐ Yes ☐ No	☐ Yes ☐ No
	☐ Yes ☐ No	☐ Yes ☐ No
	☐ Yes ☐ No	☐ Yes ☐ No
	☐ Yes ☐ No	☐ Yes ☐ No
	☐ Yes ☐ No	☐ Yes ☐ No

CHAPTER 11

MEANINGFUL METRICS AND HOW TO USE THEM

An agile individual is empirical in their decision making.

Being empirical means making decisions based on real observations, meaningful metrics or genuine experience rather than on theory or pure logic alone.

The biggest contributor to becoming more empirical in how you operate is meaningful metrics, with meaningful being the operative word.

> IT IS A CAPITAL MISTAKE TO THEORIZE BEFORE ONE HAS DATA.
> Sherlock Holmes, (Scandal in Bohemia)

There are an infinite number of ways to measure something and come out with assessments that look like they can contribute to making a decision. My definition of a meaningful metric is one that helps you to know whether you are achieving the outcomes you are setting out to deliver.

The internet has been around for roughly thirty years now, and I'm seeing the same mistakes being made today as were made in the very beginning in how you measure the success of what you're providing online.

The classic example of this that I still see all the time is to measure 'views' on a web page. The number of views is the number of times a web page is downloaded, and it is often used as the success measure for a feature within a website.

You can think of this example as a 'vanity metric.' It makes us feel good about something we've done, but it doesn't help us to know if the feature we delivered is creating the outcome we want for our customers or if we're achieving anything that contributes to our larger goals.

Defining a metric that measures something on the way to an outcome can be effective in knowing if one specific feature is delivering value towards the larger outcome – but be careful to ensure it's not measuring something that is easy to count but is only an activity rather than a contribution to an outcome.

Let's look at an example outside technology to help clarify what I mean by vanity metrics and meaningful metrics.

Imagine your long-term goal is that by the end of 2023 you will be able to run a marathon in under 4 hours. Your

MEASURE WHAT IS MEASURABLE AND MAKE MEASURABLE WHAT IS NOT SO.
Galileo Galilei 1564 - 1642

MEANINGFUL METRICS AND HOW TO USE THEM

current best time is 5 hours and you've set targets that improve on that each month by 5 minutes. If you achieve each monthly goal, you'll achieve your long-term goal well before 2023, but you expect that shaving 5 minutes off your time will get more difficult the more you train, so the end of 2023 is still quite aspirational.

Measuring the time it takes to run a marathon is your 'one metric that matters:' whatever you do each month to improve your performance can be measured by how much it contributes to that number. The time it takes you to complete a marathon is a meaningful metric.

Measuring how often you go training might be something you do for a month or two to see if you can improve your rate of training. Combined with how long it takes to run the marathon, this measures an activity that contributes to your overall goal. The frequency of your training is a meaningful metric.

Measuring the applause you get when you cross the finish line feels good: it allows you to compare how the crowd feels as you complete a marathon. But the feeling of the crowd doesn't measure your progress towards the outcome or your activity that contributes. The applause from the crowd is a vanity metric.

Another important aspect of how to use metrics in meaningful ways is to be sure you understand the difference between measures and targets.

A measure is something that allows you to know how something is progressing in a way that helps you to plan improvements.

> WHEN A MEASURE BECOMES A TARGET, IT CEASES TO BE A GOOD MEASURE.
> Marilyn Strathern
> (paraphrasing Goodhart's law)

A target is something that allows you to know when an objective has been achieved.

Never set a measure as a target. It will not provide a meaningful target and will lose all effectiveness as a measure.

The example of this most often cited is the bounty placed on cobras by the British when they ruled India. The outcome they sought was to reduce the number of cobras, so they implemented a reward for every cobra killed. This inadvertently caused their measure to become a target. Once it was a target, it lost all effectiveness as a measure. People soon realised that they could make money by raising cobras to kill and hand them in for the reward. The result of turning the measure into a target was an **increase** in the number of cobras.

Activity

Think about the measures in your life. Maybe you have KPIs in your work, or you're working towards a personal goal. What are the measures? What type of measures are they?

MEANINGFUL METRICS AND HOW TO USE THEM

Vanity Metrics	Meaningful Metrics	Targets

CHAPTER 12

Fail Fast

An agile individual knows it is better to try something small that fails than to wait until we have something perfect to try it out.

I really don't like the phrase, "Fail Fast." It sounds like it's OK to fail and we should fail faster if we want to be agile.

I'd prefer if we called it "Learn fast," because that seems like a better description for the underlying intent.

> SUCCESS CONSISTS OF GOING FROM FAILURE TO FAILURE WITHOUT LOSS OF ENTHUSIASM.
> Winston Churchill

I've seen leaders get frustrated with this phrase because they feel we should be working to succeed at whatever it is we're doing, and this phrase is an invitation to fail.

Therein lies the irony in this phrase, because everything about failing fast is directed towards succeeding! The difference is that we acknowledge we cannot know everything up front because we are yet to learn the lessons that will arise along the way, so we want to maximise learning as we go. If we can try out something small and it doesn't have the intended outcome, we have learnt something with a small investment of time, money and effort.

The alternative to fail fast is failing slowly. This happens when we wait until we have everything in place before we try anything out and the only chance to learn if we're going in the right direction is after we've invested a lot of time, money and effort. Not only is the learning much smaller, but it only happens after we have been travelling in the wrong direction for a long time and it may be too late to change course.

I've worked on projects before the days of agile where we didn't deliver value in small pieces so we could learn, and instead delivered a complete solution after months or sometimes more than a year of effort that ended up missing the mark altogether.

One project that stands out was around building a system for a marketing department at a major insurance company – they'll remain unnamed, but they certainly weren't the only organisation working in that way in those days.

Having spent more than 6 months designing and documenting the perfect solution and another 6 months building it, we discovered that the marketing team we were building it for had become

FAIL FAST

sick of waiting and purchased a system off the shelf that provided what they needed, and the entire project was a complete waste of time.

It's true to say that one of the significant failures in that project was that we didn't engage with them throughout the work. If we had, we would have known the inevitable changes in their context before we emerged months later with our solution. The biggest failure was in not learning as we went.

By delivering something small with the intent of learning more about what was really needed, we would have remained engaged with the marketing team, they would have seen that we were making progress, and we could adapt and adjust together as we went.

One of the problems overcome by a 'fail fast' approach is the gulf between imagination and reality.

When people ask for something, they don't know how to do it themselves. They aren't imagining the outcome in the same way as the people who will do the work. They can't: they simply don't know what is involved in doing it or how it will look.

> PEOPLE DON'T KNOW WHAT THEY WANT UNTIL YOU SHOW IT TO THEM
> Steve Jobs

If you go away for a period of months with no communication or progress updates, their imagination diverges even more from the reality of what you will create.

When you reappear at the end of the work and say, "Ta-daa, look what we made!" they will often be disappointed because it isn't what they had in mind.

I've seen many times where the problem space cannot be explored effectively by gathering requirements. You can find out what people think a process is or how they describe what they need, but you will often miss areas you don't know to ask about because you don't know what they really need, and they don't know what's possible.

Case studies: voice of the manager, voice of the customer

Asking more questions at the beginning only uncovers the areas that are obvious and that you know to ask about. One eye-opening example that I will always remember was delivering an e-Commerce solution at a major beverages company. When demonstrating the end product to the manager leading that area, he pointed out that it didn't do a number of things he expected and some of the things it did do were not operating as he had imagined them to. I pointed out the requirements documentation that we had spent months defining together and that he had 'signed-off.' The solution aligned exactly to what was in the document at which point he exclaimed, "I know it's what I asked for, but it's not what I meant!"

Contrast the previous example with another outcome from a significant project in a major insurance company.

FAIL FAST

The underlying outcome we sought was to provide a simpler, easier way for people to purchase insurance products online. We had identified that a lot of people got part-way through the process and abandoned it.

A few projects had already attempted to achieve the same outcomes, but had failed to deliver. So we decided to talk to some real customers to learn more and hopefully avoid some of the mistakes from the past.

We started out by establishing a vision for what we were setting out to achieve and defining several personas for the people this would serve – including those who purchased directly and those who purchased through a sales agent and the sales agents themselves.

With an idea of who this would serve, we used the 'voice of the customer' approach and conducted dozens of interviews with customers and sales agents.

We learned immediately that our assumptions on why people were abandoning the process were entirely wrong and the thinking about what we needed to do to make it easier would not have solved the problem at all.

Based on that learning, we realised that we needed to simplify the product not the system. Changing the product was not a small task so we decided to proceed in the meantime with some small changes in the existing system that would generate at least some of the benefit.

Our next step was to use the 'paper prototyping', showing people drawings of what we intended to change and carefully observing their reactions.

> FAILURE IS SIMPLY THE OPPORTUNITY TO BEGIN AGAIN, THIS TIME MORE INTELLIGENTLY.
> Henry Ford

We learned that with some small changes we would be able to simplify the process in a way that encouraged more people to complete the purchase, even before we enhanced the product.

Before leaping into changing the system, we built a better prototype. This felt like the system, but wasn't truly functional, in that it didn't perform the sale and used 'dummy' data.

The better prototype allowed us to refine what we were planning to do, focusing the changes on what was most impactful in uplifting the customer experience and we proceeded with a much smaller project to enhance the existing system. The result was enormously more beneficial at a significantly reduced cost, delivered in less than a quarter of the time.

Many of the people caught up in their traditional thinking around how to go about projects were scornful in their discussions about what was intended. More than once it was described as, "putting lipstick on a pig," and we would not achieve anything because we were retaining the current system and only making small enhancements while the prevailing thinking dictated that the system needed to be replaced.

We eventually did proceed with the larger project, but the strategy for learning quickly meant we approached it very differently and were able to deliver much more than was originally planned at a much smaller investment.

This is just one example where a learning-first approach allowed a small team to deliver a significant result by trying small things and learning as we go along, always being ready to test our assumptions and be proven wrong.

> ANYONE WHO HAS NEVER MADE A MISTAKE HAS NEVER TRIED ANYTHING NEW.
> Albert Einstein

See the previous section on experimentation for a great way to apply fail fast to your work.

Activity

Apply a fail fast approach to something big you are working on.

As with experimentation, you first need to consider what is at risk and what assumptions you hold. You can then define something small to test those risks and assumptions. If it fails, it is only a small failure and not a failure of the whole thing.

Write down the big thing you are working on and the outcomes you are looking to achieve in the table below.

You can then ask yourself some questions about the big thing itself and its individual outcomes:

- What could go wrong?
- What if any one component of the solution fails?
- Are we assuming this is the underlying problem? How do we know?
- Will our output solve the underlying problem? How do we know?
- Is this something our customers want? How do we know?
- Is the outcome the most valuable outcome for our customers? How do we know?
- What do we know about the customer's situation? How do we know these data points are not assumptions?

List out the risks and assumptions that emerge.

Which risk or assumption is the most impactful? If you're doing this for real then you would want to assess all your risks and assumptions against each other to understand which is most impactful, but for this exercise a subjective assessment is fine, so just give them a number relative to each other. Enter this into the 'Rank' column and pick the one that ends up with the highest rank.

What small thing can you do to test that risk or assumption?

FAIL FAST

Something big I'm working on	

Rank	Risks and Assumptions

One small thing I can do to test the riskiest risk or the biggest assumption

CHAPTER 13

Continuous Improvement & Compounding Interest

Continuous improvement is the ongoing practice of adding small, incremental improvements to a product, process, or way of working. While the idea of continuous improvement is most often applied to work and products, it is equally valuable when applied to yourself.

Continuous improvement has been heavily incorporated in Lean processes where it has become a mantra for just about everything people do. In Lean processes continuous improvement is known by the Japanese term 'Kaizen' which literally translated means "change for the better".

Originating in the USA during the Second World War, the practice that would become Kaizen involved small improvements utilising existing workforce and materials due to the fact that there simply wasn't the time or additional materials to support large innovations to production processes. The practice came to Japan during the occupation by US forces after the end of the war as part of the Training Within Industry programme. Later, it became one of the foundations of the Toyota Production System, fuelling their rise from a small relatively unknown vehicle manufacturer to the largest on the planet. Continuous improvement, and Kaizen, is often credited to Toyota.

The idea behind continuous improvement is simple enough: just keep adding small improvements and over time these improvements compound into significantly better outcomes. A lot of people struggle to maintain a focus on continuous improvement because they have not practiced it enough for it to become a part of their DNA and they don't see enough improvement early on to motivate them to continue with it.

At its simplest, continuous improvement is a short, repeated cycle of inspecting and adapting.

CONTINUOUS IMPROVEMENT & COMPOUNDING INTEREST

Inspect everything. Observing how you are being, feeling and working, reflecting on what you have been doing and how you've been interacting with the people around you. Inspecting everything means that everything is open to inspection. It doesn't mean you should inspect everything at the same time, as this will only dilute your focus and provide so many potential areas for improvement that it will lead to confusion and a difficulty in prioritising which of the improvements identified should be actioned first.

Adapt everything based on those observations and reflections. Nothing nor nobody is perfect, and it would be a terrible thing if something ever was perfect, everything can be improved. As with inspection, adapting everything doesn't mean adapting everything at once. Be selective and adapt only the improvements that are most valuable. Trying to adapt too many things at the same time will make it difficult to know which improvements have worked and which should be reverted.

Continuous improvement is a mindset that believes deeply that no matter how good something is, it can still be improved. In order to develop a mindset for continuous improvement, it can help to learn some principles and simple processes you can follow to get started. Over time, continuous improvement will become second nature and small incremental improvements will emerge with less and less effort.

Plan -> Do -> Check -> Act

In Lean processes, the most popular approach for achieving continuous improvement is the "Plan-Do-Check-Act, (PDCA,) cycle," also known as the Deming cycle (named after American engineer William Edwards Deming who introduced it to Japan). It is an ongoing cycle that never ends, building small improvements over time that accumulate to significant improvements.

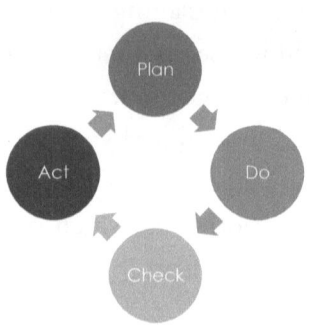

Plan

The Plan phase is where you define the outcome you seek that will deliver an improvement. Make sure you define an outcome rather than an output. The outputs will be defined when you break down what you need to do to create the outcome. Very often, people confuse the output with the outcome. An output is easy to see and define: it is the 'what' of what you will deliver. But the outcome is much more important as it defines the 'why' of what you are looking to achieve.

To provide an example of outcome vs output, you might identify that your busy work schedule has left you with little or no time to learn and feel that reading one book a month will create the learning opportunities you want to bring into your life. Increase learning opportunities is the outcome, reading books is the output. Taking it one step further – because we want our outcomes to be small, independent, and specific – you might decide that you want to learn more about golf.

If you start with the output, then it would seem easy to define a success measure as one book per month, but this will not necessarily help you to choose the right books and you may end up reading books that only reinforce existing knowledge rather than books that bring you learning.

Starting with the outcome, you will define a different success measure. It will almost always be more difficult to define success measures for outcomes because they are not as tangible as outputs, but it is well worth the effort as it helps you to be more specific and more effective when choosing the steps you will take to deliver the outcome.

For our example where you want to increase learning opportunities, let's assume they should be in the realm of improving your golf game. You might define a success measure that is much more specific to the things you want to learn, not just learning itself which would leave you with a very subjective success measure. You might define your success measure as an ability. This could form the "I'll know this is true" part of your hypothesis.

With clarity over the outcome you seek, you break it down to individual objectives and the steps necessary to deliver the expected results.

BE AGILE

During the planning phase, you want to get very explicit about the intended outcomes and how you will measure them. Setting a hypothesis will ensure it can be measured and that it becomes a learning opportunity even if it does not work out as intended.

One of the key things to keep in mind is that each improvement needs to be small and independent. Substantial changes will require more time to implement and your improvements will arrive in infrequent bursts, so it will not be continuous. Changes that are not independent will make it hard to know which of the improvements created the result.

In addition to being small and independent, each change also needs to be something that can be undone if it has unforeseen negative impacts. This can be tricky, but it is a lot easier if the change is small and discreet. Large or interrelated changes are much more difficult to reverse if they go wrong.

Returning to our example and the hypothesis you might define in that situation, using a simple hypothesis template – (I believe that <output> will create <outcome> within <time frame>. I will know this is true when <success measure>,) – you might end up with something like this:

> *I believe that reading one book a month about golf will create opportunities to learn about the tee off and improve my game within 3 months. I'll know this is true when my handicap goes from 28 to 24.*

See the section on experimentation for more details on creating a hypothesis.

Do

With a solid plan in place for the steps you need to take to create a small, measurable improvement with a clear goal, you move to the Do phase.

The Do phase is exactly as it sounds: you simply do the things you set out to do in your plan, ensuring that the capability and processes necessary to measure the outcome are in place.

If at all possible, you want to do a subset of what you have planned, rather than implementing the whole thing. That way, you reduce the impact if something goes wrong. If, as in our example, you were planning to read golf books, you wouldn't commit to buying 12 months' worth of books – you start by purchasing just one. That way, if it doesn't bring about the sought-after improvements, you haven't invested too much into it.

During the Do phase, it is important to keep reviewing the plan as you go, especially if there are multiple steps in your plan. Each step is an opportunity to review the plan and potentially modify the detail of what you are doing and what you will do next.

Check

Having done what you planned to do, the Check phase is where you check whether or not you achieved what you set out to achieve and review the success measures defined in the Plan phase.

Check phase does not suggest a dogmatic adherence to the pre-defined plan. You may not have impacted the success measure by as much as you hoped, but you may still have improved it somewhat.

If the success measure shows that there has been an improvement, then you update your understanding of the current state with the new current state, and proceed.

If you find that the experiment resulted in a deterioration of your success measure, then you leave the current state as it is and undo the changes that were the result of the experiment defined in the plan phase.

Act

The act phase is where you act to make a proven improvement a part of your standard way of operating.

By now, you've identified a potential improvement and defined a plan to test it out. You tested it in the real world, (hopefully on a small subset of everything,) and you then ran the test capturing the success measures as you went. Most recently, you checked whether the success measures were impacted as expected and determined if the change created the outcomes sought or not.

If the success measures were positively impacted, (even if they were impacted by less than you hoped, it is still an improvement,) then you want to build that change into your normal way of operating as part of the act phase.

Now that it is a part of your normal way of operating, you can 'do' the change across any remaining areas, all the time keeping an eye on your success criteria to see if any other subsets respond differently.

With that change embedded, it is time to look for the next improvement. This is, after all, intended to be continuous improvement. This is where many people drop the ball. It takes effort and focus to make sure you return to planning the next improvement. It can be tempting to feel that you are done, especially after a change that is successful.

Each time you go through the Plan –> Do –> Check –> Act cycle, it is important to go through each step in the process. Taking shortcuts might seem more efficient, particularly if it feels like the change is thoroughly understood and the impact is very predictable. Many people mash phases together and neglect implementing the change in a small subset of their overall operation. That means that the only opportunity to check whether the change has had a positive impact is after the whole change is in place, at which time it can be much more difficult to back out.

BE AGILE

A Daily Learning Loop – Keep a Journal

Keeping a journal is a lot like writing a diary and is fabulous way to build a habit around reflection and implement a learning loop.

Journaling helps you to capture learnings, work through problems, and express feelings you might not feel comfortable sharing with another person. It helps you to collect your thoughts and encourages looking at things from different viewpoints.

There are no rules when you are writing your journal. However you wish to express yourself or dig deeper into your thoughts is fine. Maybe you like to write in prose, compose poems, draw pictures, create mind-maps, or merely scribble. The best thing is whatever will help you express yourself.

Here are a few pointers that will help:

- Journal every day. Even if it is just a few minutes every day. You might find it useful to set aside the same time each day and write in the same place. This will help you form a habit of writing in your journal regularly.
- Keep it low-tech. Buy the nicest journaling book and pens you can find. It's perfectly okay to keep your journal in a computer file or on your phone or tablet, but writing by hand with a special pen in a beautiful journal enhances the way your mind engages with the activity and you'll find yourself expressing things more intensely.

- Use colour. Using colour enhances the way the mind interacts with the material and will improve your ability to compose and remember what you write.
- Make it easy. Always keep your journal nearby. When a thought or inspiration arises, you can jot a quick note, even if you wait until your journaling time to flesh it out.
- Write whatever comes to mind. There is no need to follow any defined structure. Let your creativity flow. Don't worry about spelling, grammar or sentence structure, and most importantly, don't worry about what others will think.

A Weekly Learning Loop - Schedule a Personal Reflection

Putting a regular personal reflection into your calendar will help you to build a habit around continuous improvement and learning. Schedule it for a time when you are not likely to have to book other things or have demands placed on your time by other people, I have mine scheduled for 15 minutes at 4:45 every Wednesday, but you might need to make it earlier or later in the day so that it works with whatever else you regularly have in your schedule.

If something arises that requires you to do something else at that time, be sure to move it rather than cancelling it.

You will need to stick to the personal reflection for a few weeks before you see any great benefits coming from it and it feels natural. The rewards are immense though: not only will you start to see improvements in how you get stuff done and how you relate to people, providing you with improved outcomes and stronger relationships, you'll feel an enhanced sense of confidence and capability as each small, individual improvement adds to your existing abilities.

As the benefits start to accumulate and you begin to feel good about it, it will get easier to stick to the time, but early on you will need to make a commitment to yourself to continue with it even if it feels difficult and a waste of time. Before you know it, you'll be looking forward to your reflection time and enjoying the process for its own sake.

When you sit down to reflect on how you've done during the previous week, here are some things to consider to help you get the most out of it:

- Make it the same day and time every week. Move it if you must, but don't cancel it.
- Choose a safe, comfortable space without too many distractions. This can be tricky if you have children, so it might be easiest if you set the time for after they are in bed.
- Use Post-It® Notes to capture your thinking. Write each individual item on its own Post-It Note so that later you can group them together, sort them and organise them in various ways.
- Review your journal entries for the last week. This will remind you of the smaller reflections you had throughout the week.

- Review your schedule from the previous week. This will remind you of the meetings and other events that occurred.
- Review your sent emails – just a quick scan of the subject line to remind you of the interactions you had outside meetings and events.
- Consider what you created or contributed to.
- Reflect on how you worked during the week:
  - What were the highlights?
  - What worked out really well?
  - What was difficult or created difficulty for others?
  - What did you learn through doing that work?
- Consider your interactions with other people.
  - What interactions went well?
  - What interactions were stressful? For you or for the other person?
  - What did you learn through interacting with others?
  - What did you help others to learn?

You will find that there are a number of things that went well and a number of things that didn't go so well. Do not dwell on the negatives that emerge. This exercise is not about finding ways to feel bad about yourself or your performance. It is about finding ways to improve.

The next step is to group associated things together. Are there connections between different things you have identified that went well or otherwise? Physically move the Post-It Notes around so that associated items are next to each other. Take a step back. Consider: what do the groupings evoke for you?

Now it is time to prioritise what you have captured. Which of the groupings or individual Post-It Notes offer the greatest opportunity for improvement? The number of Post-It Notes in a grouping is not what you are prioritising based on. Just because something has more ideas connected to it, it may not be the greatest opportunity for improvement. Look for the area that you feel would have the greatest impact on your performance, either in your work or your relationships.

Be sure to include the positives in your prioritisation. Maybe there is something that worked out really well, but you are not applying it consistently. This could be your best candidate for an improvement action.

An effective way to start your prioritisation is to first eliminate any items that obviously are not candidates for improvement. Maybe they represent trivial aspects of your work and relationships. Just remove them so they are not a distraction and reduce the number of things you need to think about.

It may be helpful to move the Post-It Notes around again, using a left-to-right or top-to-bottom organisation to identify your priority. Doing this allows you to get very specific in setting the priority for each item. Rather than having to decide which is the most important by holding them all in your mind at the same time, you can assess each one against only one other item at a time. Starting with any item, place it somewhere near the middle of your horizontal or vertical prioritised list. Take the next item and assess it against only the item you already placed. Would improving that area of your work or relationships be more impactful to your performance or less? Position the new Post-It Note accordingly relative to the first one. Move to the next Post-It Note, assess it individually against each of the other two already placed and again position it accordingly, moving the others about if necessary to make space.

Continue going through each of your Post-It Notes, assessing them against one item at a time in the already prioritised list so you can position them all relative to each other based on how impactful it would be to improve that area.

You now have a single horizontal or vertical list of things that went well or did not go well, prioritised for the opportunity they represent.

Now is the time to focus all your attention on the highest priority item. Remove the rest in order to provide that focus. What is the underlying reason for the item you chose? Why is it an issue? Or why did it go well? The thing to improve is the root cause for the item, not necessarily the item itself. Some things are very obvious, and you will not need to put too much effort into identifying the underlying causes, but most things are not so clear and the reason behind them needs to be identified.

Even if the item appears to be obvious, investing the time to think about what causes it will give you a clearer idea of what needs to happen to influence it, whether it is a difficulty that you want to alleviate or an asset that you want to enhance.

BE AGILE

Activity

Establish a cadence of personal reflection.

Considering your commitments and your lifestyle, select a short time slot that you can dedicate to reflection and journaling every day. Choose a time you can stick to. Block it out in your schedule as a recurring event so you get a reminder every day to reflect and journal.

For me this is 15 minutes at the end of every day. I've scheduled that in my calendar as, "Capture learnings for the day," and I don't consider my work day to be over until I've reflected and journaled for the day.

Daily journaling and reflection time	Scheduled
	☐ Yes ☐ No

Book a longer block of time for a weekly reflection.

Weekly reflection time	Scheduled
	☐ Yes ☐ No

I use 15 minutes on a Wednesday to reflect on the week overall. I review my daily journal entries and reflect on progress and learnings towards my goals and longer term outcomes and outputs.

CONTINUOUS IMPROVEMENT & COMPOUNDING INTEREST

Book a recurring block of time for a reflection on your way of working and your way of being.

Review and reflection of my way of working	Scheduled
	☐ Yes ☐ No
Review and reflection of way of being	Scheduled
	☐ Yes ☐ No

You might choose to re-purpose your weekly reflection once a month to focus more on how you work and your state of being. Review your journal for behaviours and interactions that were specific to day-to-day events and consider what they mean for the longer term.

CHAPTER 14

DELIBERATE PRACTICE

An agile mind needs exercise.

Just like your other muscles, your mind atrophies when it is not used and it gets stronger with exercise.

Deliberate practice involves choosing something small, simple and repeatable that contributes to your mastery of a skill or capability.

Mastery of any activity requires extensive and intense practice – but not just any practice. Deliberate practice is purposeful and systematic. Rather than merely repeating an activity over and over again until you become good at it, deliberate practice sets specific, small, short-term goals aimed at improving your performance, that are achieved through focusing your attention on that one element of the larger skill you wish to master.

BE AGILE

In the original Karate Kid movie from 1984, Daniel, the bullied teenager, (Ralph Macchio,) does not understand what he is learning when Mr. Miagi, (Pat Morita,) tasks Daniel with washing his car. He can't see how it contributes to the skill he wishes to master, (karate,) and feels that it is merely forced labour.

As Daniel is washing Mr. Miagi's car, he must put the wax on the car with clockwise movements of his right hand and take the wax off the car with counter clockwise movements of his left hand. Mr. Miagi keeps repeating, "Wax on, wax off," demonstrating the movements so Daniel can see how the practice must be performed.

What Daniel does not grasp at the time is that Mr. Miagi is training him through the deliberate practice of various karate movements. The movements don't individually represent mastery of karate, but each one brings Daniel closer to mastery. When Daniel competes at the all-valley tournament, he is very effective at using the wax on and wax off movements to block his opponent's attacks.

Another great example of deliberate practice is golfer Ben Hogan, one of the greatest golfers of the 20th century. Ben broke down every aspect of his golf swing into the smallest possible parts, devising specific methods to improve just one piece at a time which he would test for hours on end.

Each element Ben tested would be repeated until it was either abandoned as unfit to improve his golf swing or incorporated into his

DELIBERATE PRACTICE

game. By practicing small elements over and over again, Ben built up a muscle memory for each element to the point that they could be repeated exactly without needing to invest as heavily in concentrating on the small elements which freed him up to focus on his overall game.

Ben loved to practice. He would often be seen at the practice tee from sunrise to sunset with only short breaks, tirelessly repeating the same aspect of his swing until it had become a natural movement before moving on to the next small thing to improve.

After years of deliberately practicing the tiniest elements of his golf swing, retaining those methods that worked and eliminating those that did not work, he developed one of the most superbly tuned golf swings of anyone on the golfing circuit, breaking records and setting a new standard.

Activity

Thinking about something you are trying to master, what small simple goals can you set that will improve your overall performance?

Note down the skill or capability you wish to improve, the small goals that will improve your performance at that skill or capability and the activity that will achieve those small goals.

BE AGILE

Skill or capability you wish to master

Small goal that contributes	
Activity that will achieve the small goal	

Small goal that contributes	
Activity that will achieve the small goal	

Small goal that contributes	
Activity that will achieve the small goal	

Summary – Doing Agile

In this section, we've covered a wide range of tools and techniques that help you to approach your work in more agile ways. It is not exhaustive, but hopefully it is helpful.

Setting Goals.

We reviewed the importance of setting goals and a values-based approach to goal setting that makes them more compelling and more motivating. We also covered a structured approach to goal setting and introduced a goal setting canvas. In the activity at the end of this chapter, you completed a goal setting canvas for yourself.

Backlogs

Backlogs help us in maintaining a list of what we need to do to deliver on our goals. Using that for planning with lots of detail for the things we're doing next and less detail as they get further into the future. At the end of this chapter, you created a backlog of personal work items, broke them down into small achievable outcomes and then prioritised them.

Estimation

We looked at the benefits of relative estimation over time bound estimation and the cone of uncertainty. The further away the work is, the less certainty we can have that nothing will change before we get around to doing it. The need for honest forecasts that take into account the complexities yet to emerge is handled by deriving the time based on past experience with similar work. We concluded this chapter by creating a log of upcoming work that you can use to sense how accurate your time-based estimates are.

Prioritisation

Once we have a backlog of the work we need to do, we need to prioritise it, so we know we're always working on the most important and most valuable work. We used a relative importance and effort mapping exercise to enable prioritisation decisions. You assessed your own work for relative effort and importance using the same mapping technique.

Experimentation

Remembering our discussion on experimentation will help you determine how to define any work as an experiment and how to establish a 'north star' for larger work items that you can then break down into a series of small safe-to-fail experiments that allow learning and course correction. We introduced the experiment canvas and the experiment iterations canvas.

You utilised the experiment canvas to define and conduct an experiment for something you are working on.

Make work visible

We looked at the importance of making work visible for being able to see what's going on in the system and how a Kanban board can be used to show the flow of valuable customer outcomes. You created a Kanban board for your own work with WIP limits so you can draw insights about your work, your constraints and waste in the system.

Incremental and Iterative.

Breaking work down into small pieces allows you to incrementally improve something through a series of short iterations allows you to be more agile in how you do your work.

The activity for this chapter involved breaking down one of your larger objectives so you can approach it more incrementally and complete the work in iterations.

Outcome over output

Understanding the importance of delivering outcomes with as little output as possible changes the way you think about your work and drastically improves the value you deliver.

You assessed your current backlog of work to see if you are working towards outcomes or merely delivering outputs. You defined what the outcome could be for each output so you can see how you might approach it differently.

Timeboxing

Timeboxing is a technique where you set a period of time in which to do something, knowing that you won't get it all done, but will likely get the most valuable elements completed. Timeboxing is an application of the Pareto Principle, or the 80/20 rule.

You defined a timebox for an upcoming piece of work. Once completed you reflected on how it changed your thinking about the outcome when you constrained it with a timebox.

SUMMARY - DOING AGILE

Stop starting and start finishing

Limiting work in progress and focusing on one thing at a time increases flow, improves quality and increases value. Context switching is incredibly costly: the more items you have in progress, the less capacity you have for each one.

In the activity for this chapter, you listed your current work and decided if it could be split into smaller items or stopped all together.

Meaningful metrics and how to use them.

We covered the difference between meaningful metrics and vanity metrics and an understanding of metrics that are measures and those that are targets.

You assessed the metrics you currently have in place to decide if they're meaningful metrics or vanity metrics.

Fail Fast.

Failing fast outlines how being comfortable with small inexpensive failures that provide learning opportunities avoids big costly failures.

At the conclusion of this chapter, you listed the risks and assumptions relating to a large item you're working on so you can do something small to test your biggest risk or assumption. Doing something small to test a risk or assumption is much safer and less impactful if it fails than leaving it until the big thing is complete.

Continuous Improvement & Compounding Interest.

Small incremental improvements add up over time to big changes. Small changes add up, just like small interest payments and compound over time. The activity for this chapter involved establishing a cadence of reflection activities.

Deliberate Practice.

Do not forget the importance of mastery and building muscle memory through deliberate and intentional practice.

By identifying something you want to master and identifying 3 small skills that contribute to it that you can mindfully and intentionally practice will help you to develop yourself towards that mastery.

How Agile am I? Worksheet

Repeat the "How agile am I? worksheet" to create a view of your agility after having read through the book.

Rate yourself once again for each area by placing a check mark where you believe you now sit between the two statements.

My purpose is clear and compelling					I don't know my purpose
My goals are clearly defined and motivating					I don't have goals
I have plans for achieving my gaols					I don't have plans for achieving my goals
My plans are high level for future work					My plans are detailed for future work, (or I don't have plans)

My high-level plans are based on outcomes				My plans are based on something other than outcomes
The outcomes in my high-level plans are prioritised				I know what I want to achieve, but it's not prioritised
I break high level goals into small simple work items				I don't break down high level goals
My plans are detailed for my current work				My work is responsive, 'putting out fires' (or I don't have plans)
I regularly review and adjust my plans				My plans are locked in, (or I don't have plans)
I regularly pause and reflect on how I'm going so I can improve				I don't reflect on how I'm going
I work on one thing at a time so I can focus				I'm always multi-tasking
I use metrics to understand and improve my performance				I don't measure my performance
I try out small things quickly rather than big things perfectly				I stick with something until it is perfect

HOW AGILE AM I? WORKSHEET

I am an agent for positive change				I value stability and am uncomfortable with change
I work at a pace I can sustain indefinitely				I'm often working long hours and sometimes feel burnt out
I try to make everything as simple as possible				I do what is asked of me without trying to find a simpler way
I invest in mastering my craft, learning is in everything I do				I don't have time for learning
I value diversity of opinion; I know I can learn from everyone				I prefer to seek the opinions of those like me

What emerges from repeating the exercise?

What is different between using the worksheet at the beginning of the book and repeating it at the end?

Have new learning opportunities emerged?

Conclusion

Agile is a mindset and a way of being.

Being agile involves everything from having a clear and compelling purpose through to how you approach the smallest tasks and everything in between. It is how you think about the value you deliver to others, how you plan the work you will do to create value for others, how you go about that work and how you learn every time you create value for others.

Doing agile involves adopting the practices of one of the many frameworks or methodologies that honour the agile manifesto. Doing agile helps with doing the work, but it won't necessarily help with everything else.

While doing the practices won't automatically make you agile, approaching them deliberately with a growth mindset will allow you to discover deeper meanings. Repeating a practice often enough, will create a penny drop moment for you, things will click together in your understanding, and you'll realise an intent behind the practice. When that happens, you'll be another step closer to **being** agile.

An agile individual is comfortable with uncertainty, values feedback and knows that planning is essential even if the plan itself is worthless and will evolve many times as we learn more.

To be agile means being comfortable with change and working to bring about good change in the world and in yourself.

Agile is about learning. An agile individual makes plans expecting to learn, they seek feedback and regularly reflect on their performance and their behaviour so they can improve.

Agile provides a myriad of tools for making sense of human systems. These mental models provide ways to see the system differently so we can be more effective.

An agile individual works to achieve outcomes not to deliver outputs. They know that the value is in the outcome while the cost is in the output, so they try to create the most valuable outcomes they can with the least possible output.

Having a clear and compelling purpose allows an agile individual to choose the outcomes they will strive for and how they will go about doing the work. Breaking your purpose down into outcomes and prioritising them gives you your long-term plan.

CONCLUSION

Breaking outcomes down into small tasks that are prioritised and can be completed quickly, gives you your short-term plans and delivers more value in the long term.

An agile individual thinks about the long term but they work in the short term.

Limiting how much work is in progress helps the agile individual to focus, get more done and reduces the cost of context switching.

Visibility and transparency in all things allows empirical decision making, faster resolution of problems and improves predictability.

Investing the time and effort in uplifting your individual agility will help to make your work flow faster, your quality improve and the value of what you do increase, but those are merely pleasant side effects.

The real benefits of becoming a more agile individual are in the way it puts the focus back on people rather than their output, in how it brings learning and growth and in the way it brings joy to every action and interaction.

My personal mission is, "To help people see differently, so they find joy!" If this book has helped you to see something in a new way that brings joy to your life, then my mission has been successful.

Go forth and BE Agile!

Still want more?

Looking to elevate the agility of your event, your organisation, your team, or yourself?

Agility talks

Terry is a seasoned speaker on everything agile who brings a unique blend of knowledge, wisdom, authenticity and humour to create impactful experiences that inspire audiences to see the world differently while learning techniques that expand their thinking and create opportunities to apply agility for their competitive advantage.

With his depth and diversity of experience, Terry brings agile to life in ways that are relatable for the audience, combining real-world experience with metaphor and stories to make learning accessible in ways that lead to genuine capability uplift and behaviour change.

Having organised conferences and events himself, he knows what it takes to make this a smooth and easy engagement for event hosts. Topics can be co-created with event organisers to suit their specific needs with activities and materials designed to suit the style and personality of your event.

Enterprise coaching

Organisations preparing for or going through an agile transformation are facing a world of uncertainty and potential risk. Not all agile transformations deliver what they set out to achieve, some deliver very little in the way of improvement and some even cause significant damage.

Terry provides an impartial viewpoint that gives senior leaders an honest assessment of where they are and how they can get to where they want to go while avoiding the pitfalls and the mistakes that are commonplace.

Whether you're starting out in your agile transformation or well down the track, a few hours with Terry can be make the difference you need to take concrete steps forward towards your goals.

Training

Online training is available for Team Leaders, Product Leaders and Team Members.

STILL WANT MORE?

Training with Terry is both enjoyable and educational. His online training courses bring agile to life in ways that are relevant and lead to true capabilities not just conceptual understanding.

Team Leaders or Scrum Masters are faced with many challenges they are not prepared for by the industry certifications. Training with Terry is a hands-on, experiential, learning journey that covers all the basics while also preparing you to be an amazing Team Leader by filling in the gaps you won't get anywhere else.

Product Leaders or Product Owners often find themselves in their role with little or no understanding of the difference between being a good Product Owner and being an amazing one. The industry certifications help them to understand the basics, but that's never enough in today's fast paced corporate environment.

Team Members find themselves thrust into agile transformations with only the most fundamental training and minimal support. Training with Terry provides not just what to do and how to do it, but also why you are doing it.

Get in touch at http://www.terryhaayema.com/

About the Author

Terry Haayema was born and raised in New Zealand. He is the 6th child out of 7 in a loving, supportive family of Dutch ancestry.

Terry started his career in sales and moved into project management in the early 1990s. He shifted from managing technology projects to software development during the internet boom delivering major projects for companies like Intel, Qantas, Channel 7, and Channel 10.

Terry took on the role of Product Owner at Coca-Cola Amatil in the late 2000s, further extending his experience with agile ways of working and broadening his abilities with product delivery and understanding of customer value.

With his breadth of experience across the delivery of technology projects, Terry moved into agile coaching in the early 2010s which he continues to this day as a senior agile coach at Australia's largest bank, Commonwealth Bank of Australia.

Terry is very active in the agile community in Sydney as one of the organisers of Agile Tour Sydney, an annual agile conference based on workshops and co-created learning experiences rather than speeches, he is also a host for the Agile Sydney User Group Meetup.

As a speaker on all things relating to agile and business agility, Terry has presented at many conferences and events around the world including Australia, USA, Europe and Africa.

As a teacher, trainer and facilitator, Terry has designed and facilitated a great many highly acclaimed learning experiences for groups of up to 1,000 participants.

He was ordained as a Buddhist Monk in Shinnyo-en Buddhism in 2015.

He lives today in Sydney Australia with his loving wife of 22 years and 2 grown sons.

www.ingramcontent.com/pod-product-compliance
Lightning Source LLC
Chambersburg PA
CBHW021138080526
44588CB00008B/117